Ultimate Survival & Wilderness Skills for Kids

Step by Step Outdoor Safety & First Aid Basics: Start a fire, Build A Shelter, and Find Water - Handle Any Situation with Confidence and Resilience!

Copyright © 2024 by JAD Publishing Ltd

All rights reserved.

No portion of this book may be reproduced in any form without written permission from the publisher or author, except as permitted by U.S. copyright law.

This publication is designed to provide accurate and authoritative information in regard to the subject matter covered. It is sold with the understanding that neither the author nor the publisher is engaged in rendering legal, investment, accounting or other professional services. While the publisher and author have used their best efforts in preparing this book, they make no representations or warranties with respect to the accuracy or completeness of the contents of this book and specifically disclaim any implied warranties of merchantability or fitness for a particular purpose. No warranty may be created or extended by sales representatives or written sales materials. The advice and strategies contained herein may not be suitable for your situation. You should consult with a professional when appropriate. Neither the publisher nor the author shall be liable for any loss of profit or any other commercial damages, including but not limited to special, incidental, consequential, personal, or other damages.

1st edition 2024

Table of Contents

Introduction — 11
The Importance of Learning Survival Skills
Strengthening Family Bonds Through Shared Learning
Overview of the Book Structure
Empowerment and Encouragement

Chapter 1: Introduction To Survival Skills — 16

Understanding Survival – Why It's Important

- Safety First – Basic
- The Importance of Adult Supervision and Communication
- How to Assess and Avoid Potential Hazards
- Staying Put if You're Lost

Staying Calm and Confident - The Power of a Positive Mindset

- Techniques for Staying Calm Under Pressure
- Visualization and Mental Preparedness Techniques
- Overcoming Fear and Anxiety: Basic Psychological Strategies

Different Environments Where Survival Skills Are Applicable

Chapter 2: Water — 30

Water: The Source of Life

- Why Water Is Important
- Finding and Purifying Water
- Finding Water Sources in the Wilderness
- Why Clean Water Is Important

How to Find Natural Water Sources

Putting Skills to Practice Project: Make an Emergency Water Filter

Boiling Water for Purification Step-by-Step

Chemical Water Treatments – Tablets and Drops

- Chemical Water Why Use Chemical Treatments for Water Purification?
- Types of Chemical Treatments

Step-by-Step Instructions for Using Water Purification Tablets

Chapter 3: Fire: A Multipurpose Survival Tool — 41

Why Fire Is Important

How to Start a Fire: Step by Step

Primitive Fire Starting Methods

- Hand Drill Method
- Bow Drill Method
- Flint and Steel
- Fire Plough
- Magnifying Glass (Solar Fire)

Putting Skills To Practice Project: Fire Starters

Using Matches and Lighters Safely

- Basic Safety Rules for Using Matches and Lighters
- How to Strike a Match Safely
- Types of Lighters and Their Uses

What Is a Rocket Stove and How Does It Work?

- How to Build a Rocket Stove Out of an Aluminum Can

Chapter 4: Foraging 57

How to Start Foraging

How to Identify Plants by Their Shapes, Colors, and Textures
- Recognizing and Foraging Edible Plants

Universal Edibility Test

Common Toxic Plants to Avoid

15 Most Common Edible Plants in the United States

Foraged Wild Food Simple Recipes

- Dandelion Leaf Salad
- Wild Strawberry and Nut Mix
- Chickweed Pesto
- Cattail Shoot Wraps
- Wood Sorrel Lemonade

Safe Foraging in Urban Areas

Chapter 5: Hunting, Fishing, and Simple Trapping Techniques 73

Materials Needed for Basic Traps

- Step-by-Step Instructions For Building A Simple Snare Trap
- Safety and Ethical Considerations for Trapping
- Types of Small Game You Can Catch with a Simple Snare Trap
- Putting Skills to Practice Project: PVC Bow for Small Game Hunting

Basic Fishing Skills

- Why Fishing Is Important
- Basic Fishing Techniques
- Cleaning and Cooking Fish

Chapter 6: Shelter 83

Shelter: Your First Line of Defense

Why Shelter Is Important

- Types of Shelter

How to Gather Materials Safely

Building Your Lean-To Shelter: Step-by-Step

Improving and Maintaining Your Shelter

Constructing a Debris Hut

Making a Snow Shelter – Igloos and Quinzees

Tools and Materials Needed

Urban Shelter Solutions – Finding Safe Spots in the City

- Importance of Urban Shelters in Emergencies
- Identifying Common Safe Spots in Urban Areas
- Making Urban Shelters More Comfortable and Safe
- Signaling for Help While in Urban Shelters

Chapter 7: Survival Gear 97

Essential Survival Gear for Different Environments

Customizing Your Survival Kit

How to Pack and Maintain Your Survival Kit

Chapter 8: Navigation and Signaling Skills 104

Understanding the Basic Parts of a Compass

- How to Hold and Read a Compass Properly

Step-by-Step Instructions for Taking a Bearing

Navigating by the Sun

Using an Analog Watch for Solar Navigation

Night Navigation – Using the Stars

- Finding the North Star (Polaris)
- Using Other Constellations for Navigation
- Creating and Following Natural Landmarks
- The Importance of Natural Landmarks in Navigation
- Creating Your Own Landmarks
- Following Natural Landmarks
- Practical Examples of Using Landmarks in Different Environments
- The P.A.U.L. Navigation Method: A Simple Way to Find Your Way

Emergency Signaling: Using Mirrors and Reflective

- Understanding Mirror Signaling
- Step-by-Step Instructions for Using a Signal Mirror

Whistle Signals – What They Mean

- The Importance of Whistle Signals in Emergencies

Creating Smoke Signals

- The Significance of Smoke Signals
- Step-by-Step Instructions for Building a Smoke Signal Fire

Making Ground-to-Air Signals

- The Purpose of Ground-to-Air Signals
- Step-by-Step Instructions for Making Ground-to-Air Signals

Chapter 9: Weather Prediction   125

Weather Prediction: Observing Cloud Patterns

- Different Types of Clouds and Their Significance
- Cloud Movement and Weather Changes
- How to Observe Cloud Formations Over Time
- Special Cloud Formations and What They Mean

Reading Animal Behavior: How Animals Can Help Predict the Weather

- How Animals Sense Weather Changes
- Observing Bird Behavior for Weather Clues
- Insects and Amphibians as Weather Indicators

Using Wind and Temperature Changes: Predicting Weather with Nature's Clues

- Understanding Wind Direction and Weather Conditions
- How Wind Speed Affects Weather Predictions
- Using Temperature Changes to Predict Weather

Putting Survival Skills To Practice Project: Weather Instruments

- Making a Simple Barometer
- Making a Rain Gauge
- Creating a Wind Vane and Anemomter

Chapter 10: Urban Survival Skills   137

Avoiding Dangers – Staying Safe in Crowded Areas

Finding Safe Places in Urban Settings

Staying Safe While Moving Through Urban

Chapter 11: Basic Self-Defense Techniques   142

Basic Self-Defense Moves

Using Self-Defense Responsibly

Chapter 12: First Aid Essentials   147

Treating Cuts and Scrapes

- Preventing Cuts and Scrapes

Dealing with Burns and Blisters

- Understanding Burns
- Treating Minor Burns
- Handling Blisters
- When to Seek Adult Help

Handling Sprains and Strains

- Understanding Sprains and Strains
- Using the R.I.C.E. Method
- When to Seek Medical Help
- Preventing Sprains and Strains

Recognizing and Treating Dehydration

- Why Water is Essential
- Signs and Symptoms of Dehydration
- Steps for Treating Mild to Moderate Dehydration
- When to Seek Help for Severe Dehydration

Recognizing and Treating Frostbite and Hypothermia

- Understanding Frostbite and Hypothermia
- Recognizing Frostbite
- Treating Frostbite
- Recognizing Hypothermia
- Treating Hypothermia
- Preventing Frostbite and Hypothermia

Nature's First Aid Kit – 25 Most Common Plants, Roots, Bark, and Berries

Chapter 13: Interactive Learning and Practice   162

Benefits of a Family Survival Weekend

- Planning Your Family Survival Weekend
- Specific Survival Challenges to Include

Reflect, Review, and Ready for Next Time

- The Importance of Debriefing and Reflection
- Discussing What Went Well and What Could Be Improved

- Sharing Individual Experiences and Insights
- Setting Goals for Future Survival Practice

Building Shelters and Fires

- Step-by-Step Instructions for Backyard Shelter Building
- How to Safely Start a Fire in the Backyard

Additional Backyard Survival Activities

Scavenger Hunts for Edible Plants

- Guidelines for Organizing a Scavenger Hunt
- Ways to Make the Scavenger Hunt Engaging
- The Importance of Reviewing and Discussing Findings

Navigation Exercises – Compass and Map Challenges

- Step-by-Step Instructions for Setting Up Navigation Exercises
- How to Use a Compass and Map Together
- Additional Navigation Challenges

True Survival Stories – Kids Who Made It

Continuous Learning – How to Keep Improving Your Skills

- The Power of Practice: Why Keep Learning?
- Everyday Practice: How to Keep Your Skills Sharp
- Tracking Your Progress: Keeping a Survival Skills Journal
- Learning from Others: Finding Mentors and Resources
- Keep Learning, Keep Growing

Fun and Safe Survival Games to Play with Friends

- Why Play Survival Games?
- Survival Games You Can Play
- Get Creative: Inventing Your Own Games
- Playing to Learn

Final thoughts for young adventurers

Final Encouragement

- A Note From The Author

Introduction

Imagine this: Ten-year-old Alex and his family set out on what was supposed to be a fun weekend camping trip. They pitched their tents, roasted marshmallows over the fire, and told ghost stories under the stars. But as night fell, a thick fog rolled in, and Alex, who had wandered a little too far from the campsite while gathering firewood, suddenly found himself lost in the dense woods. Panic set in as he realized he couldn't find his way back.

But instead of freezing in fear, Alex remembered what he had learned from his parents just a few weeks before. He stayed calm, marked his spot, and began to use the survival skills he had been taught. He found a safe spot to stay, built a small shelter from branches, and knew not to stray too far. Hours later, when his parents and a park ranger found him, they were amazed at how well he had handled the situation. Alex had turned what could have been a terrifying ordeal into a triumph of resourcefulness and bravery.

Why This Book Was Written

This story of Alex could be any child's story. The world is unpredictable, and sometimes the unexpected happens. *Ultimate Survival & Wilderness Skills for Kids* was written to prepare children for just that—to ensure that they have the knowledge, skills, and confidence to navigate whatever life throws their way. This book is here to equip children with essential survival skills that will not only help them if they find themselves in a challenging situation but will also build their levels of resilience, boost your confidence, and make them feel capable of tackling any obstacle.

My Journey and Dedication

My passion for helping kids develop these crucial skills comes from my own experiences as both a parent and an outdoor enthusiast. I remember the first time I took my kids camping. We were miles from civilization when we encountered a sudden storm. I watched as they quickly applied the skills we had practiced together—finding shelter, staying warm, and keeping calm. That moment solidified my belief that every child should have the tools to handle whatever nature or life might bring. It's not just about surviving; it's about thriving in any situation. My goal with this book is to pass on that same knowledge and passion to you.

The Importance of Learning Survival Skills

Why learn survival skills? Because they are more than just a set of practical techniques; they are life skills. Knowing how to respond in an emergency—whether lost in the woods or facing a sudden blackout in the city—can make all the difference. Studies have shown that children who learn survival skills are more confident, better problem-solvers, and more resilient in the face of adversity.

Take this into account: According to the National Center for Missing and Exploited Children, 91% of children who are found after being lost had some understanding of basic survival principles. Whether you live in an urban area or spend time in the wilderness, survival skills can enhance your safety and well-being. By the end of this book, your child will not only know how to handle the unexpected but will also have the confidence to lead others through it.

When children learn how to solve problems, make decisions under pressure, and take care of themselves and others, they develop a resilience that will serve them throughout their lives. These experiences also help to foster leadership skills, as children learn to take initiative and guide others in challenging situations.

The beauty of survival skills is that they can be introduced in simple, age-appropriate ways. Even a three-year-old can learn basic concepts like staying warm, finding safe places, or understanding the importance of water. As children grow, these lessons can evolve into more complex and hands-on activities, turning what might seem like serious training into fun and engaging family time. Whether it's a backyard camping trip, a nature walk to identify edible plants, or a practice fire drill, these moments are not just opportunities for learning but also for strengthening the bonds between family members.

In a fast-paced world where screen time often dominates, survival skills provide a valuable opportunity to reconnect with nature and with each other. They remind us of our roots, our capabilities, and the importance of working together as a family. Through the pages of this book, you and your children will embark on a journey that equips them with essential life skills while also creating cherished family memories. This journey will help them grow into confident, responsible, and capable individuals—ready to face whatever life may bring.

Strengthening Family Bonds Through Shared Learning

Reading together is a special way for you and your child to bond and share new experiences. By setting aside time to enjoy this book together, you're not only creating wonderful memories but also helping them develop important reading and learning skills.

Survival skills can be a fantastic way to bond with family and friends. Imagine working together to build a shelter or learn how to start a fire. These activities provide opportunities for shared experiences and teamwork. Learning survival skills together not only strengthens your

family bonds but also creates lasting memories. It's a chance to share knowledge, encourage each other, and celebrate your accomplishments as a team. Plus, you'll have fun discovering new things together!

By diving into survival skills, you're setting up a future filled with confidence, adventure, and meaningful connections. So, get ready to explore, learn, and have fun as you uncover the exciting world of survival skills. The journey is just beginning, and the skills your child master will make for a capable and adventurous young explorer.

Overview of the Book Structure

Survival Skills for Kids is designed to be an exciting and practical guide that teaches children aged 7-14 essential survival skills. The book is divided into clear, easy-to-follow chapters, each focusing on a critical area of survival. Here's a glimpse of what the book will cover:

- **First Aid:** Learn how to treat cuts, scrapes, and other common injuries, and understand the basics of staying healthy in the wild.

- **Shelter Building:** Discover how to construct different types of shelters using natural materials, ensuring safety and warmth in any environment.

- **Fire Starting:** Master the art of building and maintaining a fire using various methods, even in challenging conditions.

- **Water Purification:** Understand the importance of clean water and learn multiple techniques to purify water from natural sources.

- **Foraging:** Identify edible plants, fruits, and nuts in the wild, and learn the basics of foraging safely.

- **Navigation:** Gain confidence in navigating with and without a compass and learn how to find your way using natural landmarks and the stars.

- **Emergency Signaling:** Discover how to attract attention in an emergency, using both modern tools and natural resources.

Each chapter includes interactive activities, such as hands-on projects, quizzes, and fun challenges, making the learning process engaging and memorable. Whether in your backyard or out in the wilderness, these activities will help to practice and hone skills in a safe environment.

Empowerment and Encouragement

This book is more than just a guide; it's a tool to empower your children. By learning these skills, they will feel capable and prepared, knowing that they can handle unexpected situations with confidence. Survival skills are not just about being ready for emergencies—they're also about having fun, exploring nature, and developing self-reliance.

Encourage practicing these skills together, turning survival training into a shared adventure. As you learn together, you'll realize that these skills can be a fun and valuable part of life, helping you all grow into a resourceful and resilient group.

The world is full of surprises, and with the skills taught from this book, they will be ready to tackle whatever comes their way. They will be eager to share what they have learned with their friends and cousins and make survival skills a shared experience that brings everyone together.

So, let's get started on this journey together—learning, growing, and becoming capable, confident, and ready for anything!

Your Survival Kit Checklist

Make sure you keep your supplies updated and check for any expiration dates and restock as necessary.

🍎 Food and Drink

- Water
- Snacks (Dried fruit, granola bars, sweets)

🚨 Emergency Supplies

- Flashlight with Batteries
- Signaling Mirror
- Hand warmers
- Emergency Contact Numbers
- Whistle

✚ First Aid Kit

- Bandages
- Antiseptic Wipes
- Gauze
- Medicine
- Small scissors
- Sunscreen
- Plasters

👕 Extra Clothing

- Long pants
- Gloves
- Long Sleeved shirt
- Hat

🔥 Fire-Starting

- Matches
- Lighter

Other Essentials

- Compass
- Map
- Paper and Pencil
- Phone

Chapter 1
Introduction To Survival Skills

Imagine facing a challenge and knowing exactly what to do. Learning survival skills helps build your confidence. When you master the basics of starting a fire, finding food, or building a shelter, you're not just learning practical skills—you're also becoming a problem-solver. Each skill you learn adds to your toolkit, giving you the confidence to tackle new and unexpected situations. You'll start to see challenges as opportunities to apply what you've learned and grow stronger in your abilities.

Survival skills are more than just lessons—they're adventures waiting to happen! By learning how to find water, identify edible plants, or build a shelter, you're encouraged to explore the great outdoors. These skills turn a walk in the park into a thrilling quest or transform a camping trip into a hands-on learning experience. The outdoors becomes your classroom, and every adventure is a chance to practice and enjoy nature. This enthusiasm for exploring helps grow a lifelong love for nature and encourages you to stay active and engaged.

Understanding Survival – Why It's Important

> **Imagine this:** You're on a family hike in the woods, enjoying the fresh air and the sounds of nature. Suddenly, you realize you've wandered off the trail, and you're not sure how to get back. The sun is setting, and the forest seems much larger and scarier than it did just an hour ago. What would you do?

Situations like this are more common than you might think, and they highlight the importance of knowing how to survive when things don't go as planned. Survival skills aren't just for extreme adventurers or those who live in the wilderness—they're valuable for everyone. Whether you're out in the woods, facing a natural disaster, or even in your own neighborhood during an emergency, having survival skills can make the difference between safety and danger.

In any survival situation, **safety should always be your top priority.** Knowing how to stay safe can help you avoid danger and make sure you get back to safety as soon as possible. Here are some basic safety rules to remember.

Safety First – Basic

1. **Always Stay with Your Group or Within a Safe Area:**

    - If you're with other people, stick together. It's easier to stay safe and find help if you're not alone. If you need to leave the group, make sure someone knows where you're going.

    - If you're in a safe area, like a campsite or a sheltered spot, stay there unless you absolutely need to leave. Moving around too much can make it harder for rescuers to find you.

2. **Avoid Dangerous Animals and Plants:**

    - Not all animals and plants are safe to touch or eat. If you see a wild animal, keep your distance and never try to approach or feed it

    - Some plants can be poisonous or cause skin irritation. If you're unsure whether a plant is safe, don't touch or eat it.

3. **Signal for Help if You Feel Unsafe or Lost:**

    - If you're lost or in danger, make noise to attract attention. You can use a whistle, shout, or bang on something to make noise.

    - If you have bright clothing or a reflective item, wave it around so others can see you. The goal is to make yourself as visible and noticeable as possible.

The Importance of Adult Supervision and Communication

1. **Inform Adults of Your Plans and Whereabouts:**

    - Always tell an adult where you're going and when you plan to be back. This way, they'll know where to look if something goes wrong.

    - If you're going on an adventure or exploring, it's a good idea to take an adult with you. They can help keep you safe and offer advice if you encounter any problems.

2. **Use Communication Tools:**
   - Carry a whistle or a small mirror with you to signal for help if needed. A whistle's sound can travel far, and a mirror can reflect sunlight to create a visible signal.
   - If you have a phone, make sure it's charged and keep it in a waterproof bag. You can use it to call for help or share your location if necessary.

How to Assess and Avoid Potential Hazards

1. **Identifying Hazardous Terrain:**
   - Be careful of steep slopes, cliffs, or unstable ground. These areas can be dangerous to walk on and could lead to falls or injuries.
   - Avoid crossing rivers or streams if the water is fast-moving or if you're unsure of the depth. It's better to find a safe way around.

2. **Recognizing Signs of Dangerous Weather:**
   - Keep an eye on the sky. Dark clouds, sudden temperature drops, or strong winds can signal that bad weather is coming.
   - If you notice these signs, seek shelter immediately, especially if there's a chance of a storm.

Staying Put if You're Lost

1. **Make Yourself Visible to Rescuers:**
   - If you get lost, it's usually best to stay in one place. Moving around too much can make it harder for rescuers to find you.
   - Find an open area where you can be seen from the sky or from a distance. Use bright clothing, mirrors, or other items to signal your location.

2. **Conserve Energy and Resources:**
   - Staying in one place helps you save your energy and keeps you from getting more lost. If you're in a safe spot, rest and stay calm.
   - Use your supplies wisely. Don't eat all your food or drink all your water right away. Ration them so they last until help arrives.

Practical Applications and Importance of Survival Skills

Survival skills are about more than just getting by—they're about thriving in challenging situations. These skills teach us how to think clearly under pressure, make smart decisions, and use the resources around us to stay safe and healthy. In everyday life, knowing how to handle unexpected situations, like getting lost during a hike, is empowering. It helps build confidence and resilience, qualities that are useful in all areas of life.

Throughout history, there have been countless examples of people who survived against the odds because they knew what to do. From shipwrecked sailors to explorers lost in the mountains, these stories remind us that survival skills are essential for everyone. They show us that self-reliance and resilience—being able to take care of ourselves and bounce back from difficult situations—are key to surviving and thriving.

Staying Calm and Confident - The Power of a Positive Mindset

When faced with a challenging situation, your mindset can make a huge difference. Staying calm and confident can help you think clearly and make smart decisions, which is crucial for staying safe and finding solutions. Here's why having a positive mindset is so important in survival situations:

- **Better Decision-Making:** When you're calm, you can think more clearly and make better decisions. Panic can cloud your judgment and lead to mistakes.

- **Enhanced Focus:** A positive mindset helps you focus on the task at hand, whether it's building a shelter, finding water, or signaling for help.

- **Increased Confidence:** Believing in yourself and your abilities boosts your confidence, which helps you tackle challenges more effectively.

Techniques for Staying Calm Under Pressure

When you find yourself in a stressful situation, try these techniques to stay calm and focused:

- **Deep Breathing:** Take slow, deep breaths to help calm your nerves. Inhale through your nose, hold for a few seconds, and then exhale slowly through your mouth. This helps reduce stress and clear your mind.

- **Visualization:** Imagine yourself successfully overcoming the challenge you're facing. Visualizing a positive outcome can boost your confidence and help you stay focused on your goals.
- **Positive Self-Talk:** Use encouraging words with yourself. Remind yourself that you can handle the situation and that you're prepared for it.

The Calm Rescuer

The Story of Aron Ralston

Aron Ralston was a young adventurer who loved exploring the outdoors. One day, while hiking alone in a remote canyon in Utah, he faced a challenging and life-threatening situation. As he was climbing, a large boulder shifted and trapped his arm against the canyon wall.

Staying Calm in a Crisis: Example 1

Even though Aron was in a very dangerous situation, he stayed calm and focused. Here's how staying calm helped him:

- **Keeping Cool Under Pressure:** Despite the pain and fear, Aron didn't panic. He took deep breaths and tried to think clearly about his options. By staying calm, he was able to think logically about how to free himself.
- **Using Survival Skills:** Aron remembered his survival training. He knew that if he didn't act quickly, he might not survive. Using his knowledge, he carefully evaluated his situation and decided to use his tools to help himself.
- **Problem-Solving:** Aron used a multi-tool he had with him to carefully and methodically cut through the soft tissue around his trapped arm. He took his time, being as precise as possible to avoid making the situation worse.
- **Visualizing Success:** While working to free himself, Aron kept his focus on his goal: escaping and getting to safety. This mental focus helped him stay motivated and continue working even though it was a difficult task.

How Staying Calm Helped

Aron's calmness allowed him to stay focused and make thoughtful decisions. His **clear thinking** helped him use his tools effectively and manage his pain. By **staying positive** and using his survival skills, Aron was able to free himself from the boulder after several hours.

Once he was free, Aron made his way to safety and eventually reached help. His ability to stay calm under extreme pressure was crucial in this life-threatening situation.

Lesson Learned: Aron Ralston's story shows that staying calm can help you think clearly and use your skills to solve problems. In emergencies, being calm and focused is essential for making smart decisions and finding solutions.

So, remember, when faced with a tough situation, **taking deep breaths, staying focused, and using your survival skills can make all the difference**. Just like Aron, you can handle challenges effectively by keeping a positive mindset and staying calm.

The Calm Young Adventurer
The Story of Jessica Anderson

Jessica Anderson was a 12-year-old girl who loved hiking and camping with her family. One summer, they decided to explore a dense forest trail. On their hike, Jessica and her family took a break at a small clearing. While Jessica was playing near a stream, she accidentally wandered off the trail and got lost.

Staying Calm in a Crisis: Example 2

Here's how Jessica's calmness helped her:

- **Keeping Calm and Thinking Clearly:** When Jessica realized she was lost, she felt scared, but she took a few deep breaths to calm herself. Instead of panicking, she remembered the survival tips her parents had taught her. This calmness helped her stay focused on what she needed to do next.

- **Using Survival Skills:** Jessica remembered to stay put in the place where she last knew her location, as her parents had taught her that **staying in one place makes it easier for rescuers to find you**. She also knew to make her location visible, so she used her bright orange jacket and waved it to make herself more noticeable.

- **Making Safe Decisions:** While waiting for help, Jessica remembered to stay warm and hydrated. She used her knowledge to find a small shelter under some large rocks and used her water bottle sparingly, sipping just enough to stay hydrated. She also made sure to stay visible by using her jacket and making a small signal fire by safely using some dry leaves and twigs.

- **Positive Thinking:** Jessica kept her spirits up by thinking positively. She remembered her parents telling her that staying calm and hopeful increases the chances of being found quickly. This positive attitude helped her stay patient while waiting for her family and search teams.

How Staying Calm Helped

Jessica's calmness and her use of survival skills made a big difference. Her decision to stay in one place and make herself visible helped rescuers find her more quickly. By staying warm, hydrated, and positive, she maintained her strength and kept her morale high.

Lesson Learned: Jessica Anderson's experience shows that staying calm can help you remember and use your survival skills effectively. By keeping a clear head, making safe decisions, and staying positive, you can handle difficult situations better and increase your chances of getting help.

So, if you ever find yourself in a tricky situation, remember Jessica's story. Take deep breaths and stay focused.

The Story of Jason Summers and the Yosemite Cliff
The Story of Jessica Anderson

In the summer of 2016, a hiker named Jason was exploring Yosemite National Park in California. Jason, who was in his early 30s, was an experienced hiker and had taken several survival courses. During one of his hikes, he decided to take a less-traveled trail to explore a scenic overlook. Unfortunately, while climbing over some rocky terrain, Jason slipped and fell about 20 feet, landing on a narrow ledge. He was hurt but not critically injured. The ledge was precarious, and he was in a difficult spot.

How Jason Stayed Calm

- **Assessing the Situation:** Jason **remained calm** after his fall. Instead of panicking, he carefully assessed his injuries and the environment. He knew that panicking could make his situation worse. By staying calm, he was able to think clearly about what actions to take next.

- **Using Survival Training:** Jason remembered the survival skills he had learned. He used a **first aid kit** from his backpack to tend to his injuries, applying a bandage to a bleeding cut on his leg. His knowledge of first aid helped him manage his injuries until help arrived.

- **Signaling for Help:** Using his phone, Jason made sure to stay calm while communicating his location to **emergency services.** He provided clear and precise information about his exact location and the nature of his injuries. His calm communication was crucial in ensuring that the rescuers could locate him quickly.

- **Maintaining Composure:** While waiting for rescuers, Jason kept himself as comfortable as possible by **finding a safe position** on the ledge. He used his survival training to conserve his energy and stay focused on keeping himself safe.

How Staying Calm Helped

Jason's calmness and clear thinking were key to his successful rescue. By remaining calm, he was able to:

- **Assess and Treat Injuries:** He used his first aid skills to manage his injuries, preventing them from worsening.

- **Communicate Effectively:** His clear communication helped rescuers find him quickly and accurately.

- **Stay Safe:** By maintaining his composure, he avoided making the situation worse and stayed in a safe position until help arrived.

Lesson Learned: Jason's experience shows that staying calm during an emergency can make a huge difference. His ability to think clearly, use his survival skills, and communicate effectively were all crucial in ensuring his safe rescue. In any emergency, staying calm helps you make better decisions and increases your chances of staying safe and getting help.

Visualization and Mental Preparedness Techniques

Visualization and mental preparation are powerful tools for handling stressful situations. Here's how you can use them:

- **Visualizing Successful Outcomes:** Before you face a challenge, close your eyes and picture yourself successfully solving the problem. Imagine the steps you'll take and how you'll feel when you achieve your goal.

- **Mental Rehearsal:** Practice the survival skills you've learned in your mind. Picture yourself building a shelter, starting a fire, or finding food. This mental rehearsal helps reinforce your skills and prepares you for real situations.

The Role of Resilience and Adaptability in Survival

Resilience and adaptability are key to overcoming challenges. Being resilient means bouncing back from setbacks, while adaptability is about being flexible and resourceful in changing situations.

- **Practical Exercises:** You can develop resilience and adaptability through role-playing and problem-solving games. Try scenarios where you have to come up with creative solutions or make quick decisions. These exercises help build your confidence and problem-solving skills.

- **Activity Idea:** Create a "survival challenge" game with friends or family. Set up different scenarios and see how you can use your survival skills to solve them.

This will help you practice staying calm and being adaptable in various situations.

Here are some examples to get you started:

- Lost in the Woods
- Stranded in a Desert
- An Earthquake
- Lost in a City
- Stranded on a Shipwrecked Island

Overcoming Fear and Anxiety: Basic Psychological Strategies

Understanding and Managing Your Emotions

When you're in a tough or scary situation, it's natural to feel afraid or anxious. But you can learn some simple ways to help manage these feelings and stay calm. Here are some strategies to help you overcome fear and anxiety:

Identifying and Naming Your Emotions

What Am I Feeling?

- Start by paying attention to what you're feeling. Are you scared, nervous, or maybe even excited? Knowing what you're feeling can help you understand how to handle it.

Name Your Feelings:

- Once you identify what you're feeling, give it a name. For example, "I feel scared" or "I feel anxious." Naming your emotions can make them easier to manage and make you feel more in control.

Techniques for Shifting Focus

1. **Grounding Exercises** help you focus on the present moment and distract your mind from fear. Here are a few easy ones:

   - 5-4-3-2-1 Technique:
   - **5 things you can see:** Look around and name five things you notice.
   - **4 things you can touch:** Feel the texture of objects around you, like a soft pillow or a rough wall.
   - **3 things you can hear:** Listen carefully to sounds like birds chirping or the wind blowing.
   - **2 things you can smell:** Notice any scents around you, like fresh flowers or food.
   - **1 thing you can taste:** Focus on the taste in your mouth, like the flavor of a snack or the freshness of water.

2. **Breathing Exercises:**

   - **Deep Breathing:** Take slow, deep breaths in through your nose and out through your mouth. Count to four as you breathe in and again as you breathe out. This helps calm your mind and body

3. **Focus on What You Can Control:**

   - Sometimes, focusing on things you can control can help reduce anxiety. For example, if you're nervous, concentrate on what you can do to improve your situation to help soothe and clear your mind.

4. **Positive Visualization:**

   - Close your eyes and imagine a place where you feel safe and happy. Picture yourself there, feeling calm and relaxed. This can help you shift your focus away from fear and feel more confident.

Remember, It's Okay to Feel Afraid

Everyone experiences fear and anxiety sometimes. What's important is learning how to manage these feelings so you can stay calm and make good survival decisions. By using these strategies, you'll be better prepared to handle challenging situations and keep your emotions in check.

With practice, these techniques will become easier to use, and you'll feel more confident in handling any situation that comes your way. So, take a deep breath, focus on the present, and remember that you have the skills to overcome your fears.

Different Environments Where Survival Skills Are Applicable

Survival skills aren't just for the wilderness. While it's true that knowing how to find food, water, and shelter in a forest or desert is important, survival skills are also crucial in urban areas and during natural disasters.

- **Wilderness (Forests, Mountains, Deserts):** In the wilderness, survival skills help you find your way, build shelter, and stay safe from the elements. Knowing how to navigate, make a fire, and find water can save your life if you're lost in a forest or stranded on a mountain.

- **Urban Settings (Cities, Suburbs):** In cities and suburbs, survival skills might involve knowing how to find safe shelter during a power outage, where to find clean water if the taps stop working, or how to stay calm and think clearly in an emergency.

- **Natural Disasters (Floods, Earthquakes, Storms):** Natural disasters can happen anywhere, and they often strike without warning. Knowing how to prepare for and respond to events like floods, earthquakes, or storms can keep you and your family safe. This might mean knowing how to evacuate, where to find emergency supplies, or how to signal for help.

Survival Priorities – What to Focus On

When you're in a survival situation, it's important to focus on the most critical needs first. That's where the Rule of Threes comes in:

- **Three Minutes Without Air:** Breathing is the most immediate need. In a survival situation, ensuring you have access to fresh air is crucial. This could mean getting out of a smoke-filled room or staying calm if you're underwater.

- **Three Hours Without Shelter:** In harsh conditions, exposure to the elements can be life-threatening. Finding or building shelter to protect yourself from cold, heat, wind, or rain is a top priority.

- **Three Days Without Water:** Water is essential for life, and in a survival situation, finding clean drinking water is critical. Dehydration can set in quickly, so knowing how to locate and purify water is vital.

- **Three Weeks Without Food:** While you can survive longer without food than without water or shelter, you'll need energy to keep going. Knowing how to find or catch food in the wild, or how to make the most of what you have, is important for long-term survival.

Understanding these survival priorities helps you make smart decisions when you're under pressure. By focusing on what's most important, you can stay safe, keep your energy up, and increase your chances of making it through any challenge you face.

Survival skills are about more than just knowing what to do—they're about building the confidence and resilience to handle anything life throws at you.

Whether you're deep in the woods or in the middle of a city, these skills will help you stay safe, strong, and ready for anything.

When you find yourself in a survival situation, it's important to know what to focus on first. There's a simple way to remember the order of the things you need to survive, called the Basic Needs Hierarchy. This hierarchy helps you prioritize your actions so you can stay safe and healthy. Let's break down the four most critical needs: shelter, water, fire, and food.

Ultimate Survival & Wilderness Skills for Kids

Survival Priorities Pyramid

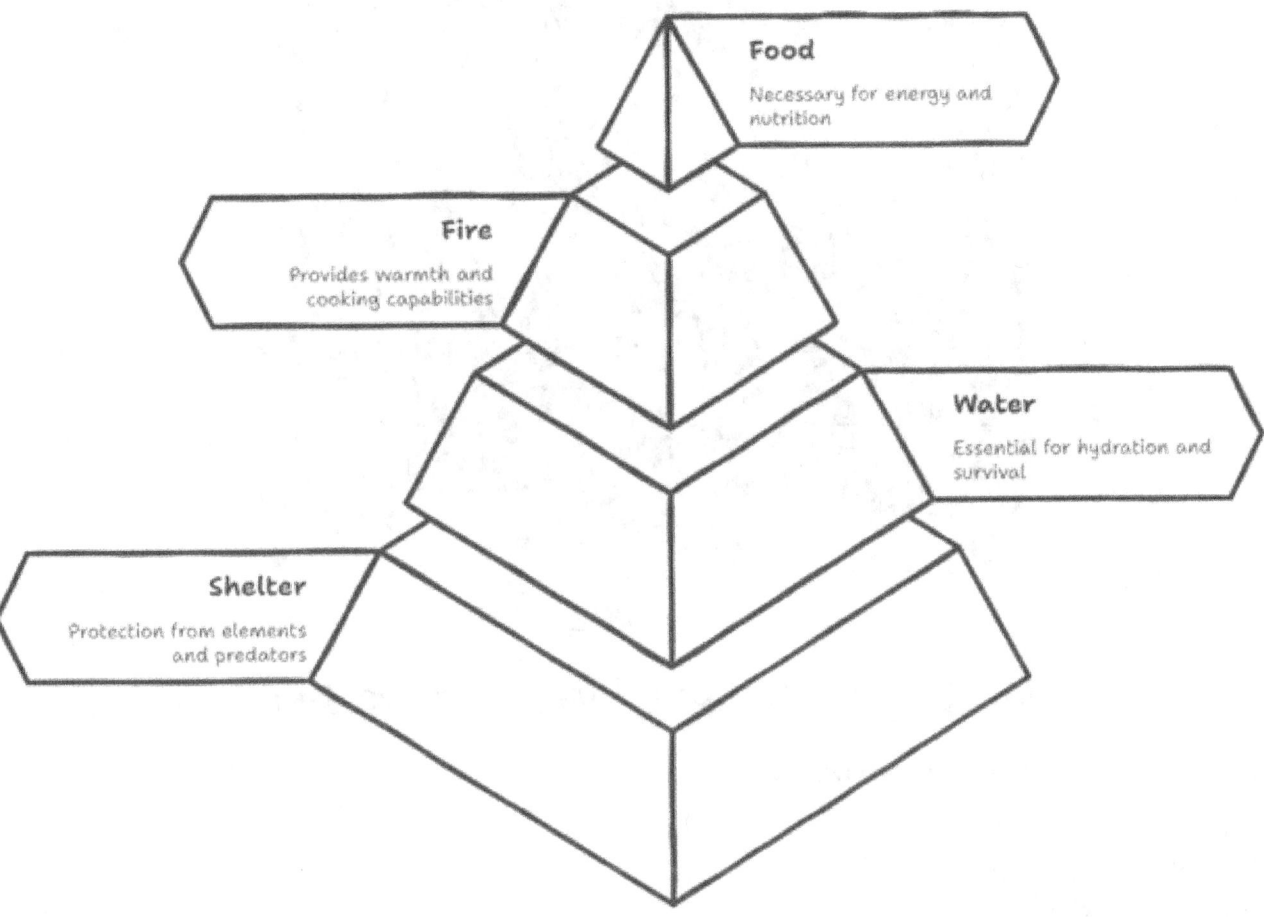

Quiz:

Chapter 1 - Introduction to Survival Skills

1. Why is it important to learn survival skills?

a) To have fun in the wilderness
b) To build confidence and become a problem-solver
c) To show off to friends
d) To avoid doing homework

2. What can learning survival skills help you become?

a) A superhero
b) A problem-solver
c) A world traveler
d) A famous chef

3. When you learn how to find food, build a shelter, or start a fire, what else are you learning besides practical skills?

a) How to make friends
b) How to play sports
c) How to face unexpected challenges with confidence
d) How to cook a gourmet meal

4. What should you do if you get lost during a family hike?

a) Run around looking for the trail
b) Yell loudly and run in the opposite direction
c) Stay calm, assess your situation, and think about what survival skills you can use
d) Sit down and wait for your family to find you

5. Which of the following is NOT a basic safety rule for survival situations?

   a) Stay with your group or within a safe area
   b) Approach and feed wild animals
   c) Signal for help if you feel unsafe or lost
   d) Avoid touching or eating unknown plants

6. Why is it important to tell an adult your plans and whereabouts before going on an adventure?

   a) So they can join you
   b) So they know where to find you if something goes wrong
   c) So they can pack snacks for you
   d) So they can tell your friends

7. What should you do if you see dark clouds and strong winds while you're outside?

   a) Ignore them and keep playing
   b) Seek shelter immediately
   c) Take a nap under a tree
   d) Start a campfire

8. Why is staying calm important in a survival situation?

   a) It makes you look cool
   b) It helps you think clearly and make better decisions
   c) It scares away wild animals
   d) It makes the situation more fun

9. What is one way to make yourself more visible to rescuers if you're lost?

   a) Hide in the bushes
   b) Stay quiet and wait
   c) Use bright clothing or reflective items to signal your location
   d) Climb the tallest tree you can find

10. Which skill is NOT mentioned as part of survival skills in this chapter?

    a) Building a shelter
    b) Identifying edible plants
    c) Navigating using the stars
    d) Cooking a meal on a campfire

Chapter 2
Water

Water: The Source of Life

After shelter, the next most important need is water. Your body can only survive for about three days without water, and dehydration can set in quickly, especially in hot or dry environments

Why Water Is Important

Hydration

Water is crucial for keeping your body functioning properly. It helps regulate your temperature, keep your organs working, and flush out toxins.

Energy

Staying hydrated helps you maintain energy levels, which is important when you're trying to survive.

Finding and Purifying Water

- **Natural Sources:** Look for streams, rivers, lakes, or rainwater. Even plants like vines or certain trees can provide water.
- **Purification:** It's important to purify water before drinking it to avoid getting sick from bacteria or parasites. You can boil water, use water purification tablets, or filter it through clean cloth.

Finding Water Sources in the Wilderness

Finding clean water in the wilderness is one of the most important survival skills you can learn. Water is essential for staying hydrated and keeping your body functioning properly.

Why Clean Water Is Important

1. **Staying Hydrated:** Your body needs water to stay healthy and energetic. If you don't drink enough water, you can become dehydrated, which can make you feel weak, dizzy, and confused.
2. **Dehydration Risks and Symptoms:** Dehydration happens when you don't have enough water in your body. Symptoms can include:
   - Thirst
   - Dry mouth and throat
   - Dark yellow urine
   - Dizziness or lightheadedness
   - Fatigue or weakness
3. **Dangers of Drinking Untreated Water:** Drinking water that hasn't been cleaned can be dangerous. It might contain bacteria, parasites, or other harmful germs that can make you sick. Always treat or purify water before drinking it.

How to Find Natural Water Sources

1. **Streams and Rivers:**

   - **Listen for Water:** Follow the sound of running water. Streams and rivers make a distinctive sound as water flows over rocks and obstacles.

   - **Look for Signs:** Look for green vegetation and animal tracks, which often indicate the presence of water.

2. **Ponds and Lakes:**

   - **Find Low-Lying Areas:** Ponds and lakes are usually found in lower areas where water collects. Look for flat or depressed land.

   - **Check the Vegetation:** Areas with lush green plants or reeds often indicate nearby water.

3. **Springs:**

   - **Find Water Seeping from the Ground:** Springs are sources where water naturally flows out of the ground. Look for wet patches or small pools of water seeping from the earth.

   - **Observe the Terrain:** Springs often occur on hillsides or in places where the ground is sloped.

4. **Collecting Rainwater:**

   - **Use Leaves or Tarps:** To collect rainwater, spread out large leaves or a tarp to catch rain. The water will then pool on the surface.

   - **Direct the Water:** If using a tarp, create a funnel by tying the edges to create a slope towards a container.

Tips for Collecting and Purifying Water

Always Purify Water: Even if you find water that looks clean, it's important to purify it before drinking. Boiling the water for at least 1 minute will kill most harmful germs. If you're at a high altitude (above 6,500 feet), boil for 3 minutes.

If you ever find yourself in a survival situation and need to clean dirty water to make it safe to drink, you can make a simple water filter using a plastic bottle and natural materials you can find around you. Here's how to do it, step by step!

Putting Skills to Practice Project: Make an Emergency Water Filter

What You'll Need:

- A plastic bottle (empty)
- A knife or scissors (for cutting the bottle)
- Small rocks or gravel
- Sand
- Charcoal - use sand if you do not have charcoal
- Grass or leaves
- Clean cloth, bandana, or coffee filter (optional but helpful)

Step 1: Prepare the Plastic Bottle

What to Do:

- Carefully cut the bottom off the plastic bottle using a knife or scissors. This will be the opening where you pour in the dirty water.

Why It's Important:

- The bottle will serve as the body of your water filter, holding all the layers of materials that will clean the water as it passes through.

Step 2: Add the Filter Layers

Now, it's time to build the layers inside the bottle. These layers will help remove dirt, particles, and some harmful things from the water.

1. Bottom Layer: Grass or Leaves

What to Do:

- Start by placing a layer of grass or leaves at the neck (the small opening) of the bottle. If you have a clean cloth, bandana, or coffee filter, you can put it here instead.

Why It's Important:

- This layer acts as the first filter, blocking large particles like leaves, twigs, and bugs from getting into your water. The cloth, if used, helps hold everything in place and catches finer debris.

2. Next Layer: Charcoal or Sand

What to Do:

- Crush some charcoal into small pieces and add it on top of the grass or leaves layer.

Why It's Important:

- Charcoal is very good at removing harmful chemicals, toxins, and bacteria from water. It also helps reduce any bad taste or smell. This is one of the most important layers for making your water safer to drink. Carrying a handful of activated charcoal capsules or chunks in your backpack is an excellent way to always make certain you are prepared for emergencies.

3. Next Layer: Sand

What to Do:

- Add a layer of sand on top of the charcoal. Make sure it's about 1-2 inches thick.

Why It's Important:

- Sand filters out smaller particles that made it through the charcoal. It's great at catching tiny bits of dirt, mud, and other impurities.

4. Top Layer: Small Rocks or Gravel

What to Do:

- Finally, add a layer of small rocks or gravel on top of the sand.

Why It's Important:

- This layer helps catch larger particles before they reach the sand and charcoal. It also slows down the water as it passes through the filter, giving the lower layers more time to clean it.

Step 3: Filter the Water

What to Do:

- Find a container to catch the clean water (like a cup or another bottle). Hold the filter over the container with the bottle's neck pointing down. Pour dirty water slowly into the open end of the bottle (the bottom you cut off earlier).

Why It's Important:

- Pouring slowly lets the water filter through each layer, giving it time to be cleaned. As the water moves down through the rocks, sand, charcoal, and grass, it should come out much clearer and cleaner at the bottom.

Step 5: Boil the Water (If Possible)

What to Do:

- If you have a way to make a fire, boil the filtered water for at least 5 minutes.

Why It's Important:

- Boiling is the best way to kill any bacteria or viruses that might still be in the water after filtering, ensuring it's safe to drink.

How Each Part of the Filter Works:

- **Grass/Leaves or Cloth:** Catches large debris and keeps the other materials in place.
- **Charcoal:** Absorbs harmful chemicals, bacteria, and bad tastes or odors.
- **Sand:** Traps smaller dirt particles and impurities.
- **Rocks/Gravel:** Filters out big particles and helps slow down the water flow.

Now you have a simple, effective water filter made from materials you can find in nature! Remember, this filter helps make dirty water cleaner, but boiling the water afterward is the best way to make sure it's safe to drink.

Boiling Water for Purification

Boiling water is one of the simplest and most effective ways to make sure the water you drink is safe. When you're in the wilderness or any survival situation, it's important to have clean water for drinking and cooking. Here's why boiling water is so effective and how you can do it yourself

Why Boiling Water Works

When you boil water, you heat it to a temperature that kills harmful bacteria, viruses, and parasites that can make you sick. These tiny organisms can be in the water even if it looks clean, so boiling is a reliable way to purify it.

- **Killing Bacteria, Viruses, and Parasites:** Boiling water destroys these harmful microorganisms, making the water safe to drink.
- **Making Water Safe for Drinking and Cooking:** Boiled water can be used for drinking, cooking, and cleaning wounds, helping you stay healthy in a survival situation.

Materials Needed for Boiling Water

To boil water, you'll need a few essential items:

- **A Heat Source:** This could be a campfire, stove, or any other way to create enough heat to boil water.
- **A Container for Boiling:** You'll need a metal pot, canteen, or any heatproof container that can hold water and withstand high temperatures.
- **Fireproof Gloves or Tongs:** These will help you safely handle hot containers without burning yourself.

Step-by-Step

1. **Collecting Water and Filling the Container:**
   - Find a source of water like a stream, lake, or rainwater. If the water has visible dirt or debris, try to filter it out using a cloth or let it settle before pouring it into your container.
   - Fill your container with the collected water but leave some space at the top to prevent it from spilling over when it boils.

2. **Placing the Container Over the Heat Source:**
   - Place your container on a stable spot over your campfire or stove. Make sure it's secure and won't tip over.
   - If you're using a campfire, position the container so it's directly above the flames.

3. **Bringing the Water to a Rolling Boil:**
   - Watch the water as it heats up. Once it reaches a rolling boil—when large bubbles are rapidly rising to the surface—keep it boiling for at least one full minute. This ensures that any harmful organisms are killed.
   - In higher altitudes, you may need to boil the water for 3 minutes since water boils at a lower temperature in those conditions.

4. **Letting the Water Cool Before Drinking:**
   - Carefully remove the container from the heat source using fireproof gloves or tongs.
   - Allow the boiled water to cool down before drinking or using it for cooking.

Practical Tips for Effective Water Boiling

- **Using a Lid to Conserve Heat:** Covering the container with a lid while boiling can help conserve heat, making the water boil faster and saving fuel.
- **Filtering Out Large Debris Before Boiling:** If the water you collected has dirt, leaves, or other large debris, try to filter it out before boiling. This can be done by pouring the water through a cloth or letting it settle and then carefully pouring the clearer water into your boiling container

---

When you're in a survival situation and need clean water, chemical treatments like tablets and drops can be a quick and easy way to make water safe to drink. Here's how they work, the different types available, and how to use them.

Chemical Water Why Use Chemical Treatments for Water Purification?

Chemical treatments are a reliable method for purifying water when you don't have access to boiling or filtering equipment. They work by killing harmful bacteria, viruses, and parasites that could make you sick if you drank untreated water.

- **Killing Bacteria, Viruses, and Parasites:** These tiny organisms can live in water and cause serious illness. Chemical treatments help make the water safe by eliminating them.

- **Portable and Easy to Use:** Water purification tablets and drops are small and light, making them easy to carry in a backpack. They're also simple to use, which is important when you're in a hurry or tired.

Types of Chemical Treatments

There are different kinds of chemical treatments that you can use to purify water. Here are some of the most common ones:

- **Water Purification Tablets:** These are small tablets that dissolve in water to kill harmful organisms.
  - **Iodine Tablets:** Effective but can leave a strong taste. Not recommended for people with iodine allergies.
  - **Chlorine Dioxide Tablets:** More effective against a wider range of organisms, including Cryptosporidium, and generally leaves less of a taste.
- **Liquid Drops:** These are small bottles of liquid chemicals that you add to water.
  - **Sodium Hypochlorite (Household Bleach):** A few drops can purify a large amount of water. Be sure to use unscented bleach.
  - **Chlorine Drops:** Similar to bleach but specifically formulated for water purification.

Step-by-Step Instructions for Using Water Purification Tablets

Using water purification tablets is easy, but it's important to follow the instructions carefully to make sure the water is safe to drink.

1. **Read and Follow the Instructions on the Packaging:**
   - Each brand of tablets may have slightly different instructions, so always read the label before using them.

2. **Adding the Correct Number of Tablets to a Specific Volume of Water:**
   - Most tablets are designed for a specific amount of water, like 1 tablet for 1 liter of water. Be sure to use the right number of tablets for the amount of water you have.

3. **Waiting the Recommended Amount of Time:**
   - After adding the tablets, close the container and wait for the chemicals to work. This usually takes about 30 minutes, but it can take longer in cold water.

4. **Shaking the Container to Ensure Even Distribution:**
   - Once the tablet is in the water, give the container a good shake to help the chemicals mix evenly throughout the water.

> ### Practical Tips and Considerations for Chemical Treatments
>
> Here are some extra tips to make sure your chemical treatments work effectively:
>
> Pre-filtering Water Before Chemical Treatment: If the water you find is muddy or full of leaves and other large particles, try to filter it before adding the tablets or drops. You can use a cloth, coffee filter, or even let the water settle so the debris sinks to the bottom.

Quiz:

Chapter 2 - Water

1. Why is water crucial for your body?

a) It keeps you warm
b) It helps regulate temperature, keeps organs working, and flushes out toxins
c) It makes food taste better
d) It helps you run faster

2. How long can your body survive without water?

a) 1 day
b) 3 days
c) 5 days
d) 7 days

3. Which of the following is a sign of dehydration?

a) Feeling very hungry
b) Dark yellow urine
c) Feeling very energetic
d) Cool and moist skin

4. What is the safest way to drink water from a natural source?

a) Drink it directly from the river
b) Purify it by boiling, using tablets, or filtering it
c) Mix it with juice
d) Add sugar to make it safe

5. What natural sources of water can you find in the wilderness?

a) Streams, rivers, lakes, rainwater, and certain plants
b) Hot springs
c) Puddles on the road
d) Bottled water

6. How do you know where to find a stream or river?

a) Look for clouds
b) Listen for the sound of running water and look for green vegetation
c) Follow animal tracks
d) Walk uphill

7. Why should you always purify water before drinking it?

a) To make it taste sweet
b) To avoid getting sick from bacteria, parasites, or other harmful germs
c) To make it colder
d) To make it more colorful

8. What should you do if your water is still cloudy after filtering?

a) Drink it anyway
b) Filter it again to make it cleaner
c) Add more dirt
d) Let it sit for a week

9. What materials can you use to make an emergency water filter?

a) Plastic bottle, rocks, sand, charcoal, grass or leaves
b) Metal spoon and knife
c) Tinfoil and paper
d) A water bottle and straw

10. How does charcoal help in purifying water?

a) It heats up the water
b) It absorbs harmful chemicals, bacteria, and bad tastes
c) It makes the water smell good
d) It turns the water black

11. What's the most effective way to purify water after filtering it?

a) Add sugar
b) Boil it for at least 1 minute (3 minutes at high altitudes)
c) Leave it in the sun
d) Freeze it

12. How long should you wait after adding water purification tablets before drinking?

a) 5 minutes
b) 10 minutes
c) 30 minutes
d) 1 hour

13. Why is boiling water a reliable way to purify it?

a) It makes the water taste better
b) It kills harmful bacteria, viruses, and parasites
c) It turns the water into steam
d) It makes the water boil faster

14. What should you avoid when collecting water in the wilderness?

a) Collecting from running streams
b) Collecting from areas near dead animals or visible pollution
c) Collecting rainwater
d) Collecting from springs

15. Why is it important to store boiled water in a clean container?

a) To make it taste better
b) To prevent it from getting contaminated again
c) To keep it cold
d) To make it last longer

Chapter 3
Fire: A Multipurpose Survival Tool

Fire is a critical survival tool that serves many purposes. Not only does it provide warmth and light, but it can also help you cook food, purify water, and signal for help

Why Fire Is Important

- **Warmth:** Fire helps you stay warm, especially at night or in cold environments, preventing hypothermia. (Hypothermia can be dangerous if our core body temperature falls to low.)

- **Cooking:** Cooking food over a fire makes it safer to eat by killing harmful bacteria.

- **Water Purification:** Boiling water over a fire is an effective way to make it safe to drink.

- **Signaling:** Smoke from a fire can be used to signal for help if you're lost or in need of rescue.

How to Start a Fire: Step by Step

Fires can be incredibly dangerous due to their potential to spread rapidly and cause severe injury or property damage. Therefore, until you feel completely confident in your abilities, it's important to have an adult present while following these steps for safety.

Starting a fire can be really useful in a survival situation. It can **keep you warm, cook your food**, and even help you **signal for help.** But starting a fire takes some practice and understanding of how it works. Here's how you can do it, step by step!

What You'll Need:

- **Dry tinder:** Something small and easy to light, like dry leaves, grass, bark, or cotton balls.
- **Kindling:** Small sticks or twigs that will catch fire from the tinder.
- **Fuel:** Larger pieces of wood that will keep the fire burning once it's going.
- **Ignition source:** Matches, a lighter, or a spark from flint and steel.

Step 1: Find a Safe Spot

What to Do:

- Choose a place to build your fire that's away from trees, bushes, or anything that can catch fire easily. Clear the ground of any leaves or grass and make a circle of rocks to keep the fire contained.

Why It's Important:

- Safety is the most important thing when making a fire. The circle of rocks helps keep the fire from spreading, and clearing the area ensures that nothing accidentally catches on fire.

Step 2: Gather Your Materials

What to Do:

- Collect your tinder, kindling, and fuel. Make sure everything is dry because wet materials won't catch fire easily. Gather more than you think you'll need, especially the kindling.

Why It's Important:

- Having everything ready before you start will make it easier to build and maintain your fire. Dry materials catch fire faster and burn better.

Step 3: Build a Fire Structure

There are different ways to arrange your tinder, kindling, and fuel, but here's a simple method:

What to Do:

- **Teepee Style:**

1. Place a small bundle of tinder in the center of your fire pit.
2. Arrange your kindling around the tinder in a teepee shape, leaving some space for air to flow through.
3. Lean the larger pieces of wood (fuel) against the kindling, also in a teepee shape.

Why It's Important:

- The teepee shape allows air to flow through the fire, which helps it burn better.
- The kindling catches fire from the tinder, and the fuel wood keeps the fire going.

Step 4: Light the Tinder

What to Do:

- Use your matches, lighter, or flint and steel to light the tinder. Hold the flame or spark close to the tinder until it catches fire. Once the tinder is burning, it will start to light the kindling.

Why It's Important:

- The tinder catches fire quickly because it's small and dry. It's the first step in building up to a bigger fire.

Step 5: Feed the Fire

What to Do:

- Once the kindling starts to catch fire, slowly add more kindling until the fire is strong. Then, start adding the larger pieces of wood, one at a time, to keep the fire burning.

Why It's Important:

- Adding too much wood too quickly can smother the fire, so add it gradually. As the fire grows, it will be able to burn larger pieces of wood.

Step 6: Maintain the Fire

What to Do:

- Keep an eye on your fire and add more fuel (large wood) as needed. If the fire starts to die down, blow gently at the base to give it more oxygen.

Why It's Important:

- Fires need three things to keep burning: heat, fuel, and oxygen. Blowing gently adds more oxygen, which helps the fire burn stronger.

Step 7: Extinguish the Fire Safely

What to Do:

- When you're done with your fire, pour water over it until all the embers are out and the ashes are cool to the touch. Stir the ashes with a stick to make sure no hot spots are left.

Why It's Important:

- Never leave a fire unattended, and always make sure it's completely out before you leave. This prevents wildfires and keeps everyone safe.

How It All Works:

- **Tinder:** Catches the initial spark or flame and burns easily to start the fire.
- **Kindling:** Burns longer than tinder and helps ignite the larger pieces of wood.
- **Fuel:** Larger pieces of wood that keep the fire going once it's established.
- **Airflow:** The spaces between your materials allow oxygen to reach the fire, which is necessary for it to burn.

Starting a fire is a valuable skill, but it's important to do it safely and responsibly.

Practice these steps, and soon you'll be able to start a fire confidently in any situation!

Putting It All Together

In any survival situation, understanding the **Basic Needs Hierarchy** helps you make smart decisions. Start by **securing shelter** to protect yourself from the elements, then find and purify water to stay hydrated. Once those are in place, focus on **building a fire for warmth, cooking, and signaling**. Finally, find and **prepare food** to keep your energy up.

By prioritizing these needs, you'll be better equipped to handle any challenge that comes your way, no matter where you are. Survival is about staying calm, thinking clearly, and taking things one step at a time—just like following the Basic Needs Hierarchy.

Ultimate Survival & Wilderness Skills for Kids

Primitive Fire Starting Methods

Hand Drill Method

This is one of the oldest and most basic ways to start a fire. It requires patience and practice but is a valuable skill.

Materials Needed:

- A dry, straight stick (spindle) about 1-2 feet long
- A flat piece of dry wood (fireboard)
- Dry tinder (like dry grass, leaves, or shredded bark)

Steps:

- **Prepare the Fireboard:** Carve a small notch near the edge of the fireboard and a small depression where the spindle will sit.
- **Set Up the Spindle:** Place the spindle in the depression on the fireboard. Hold it upright with your palms.
- **Twirl the Spindle:** Rub your hands together, rolling the spindle quickly while pressing downwards. This will create friction and heat.
- **Create an Ember:** Once you see smoke, keep spinning until a small ember forms in the notch.
- **Transfer the Ember:** Gently tap the ember into your prepared tinder nest.
- **Blow Gently:** Blow softly on the ember until the tinder catches

Safety Tip: Practice this method with adult supervision. Ensure the area is safe for fire-starting, and always have water nearby to extinguish the flames.

Bow Drill Method

A more advanced version of the hand drill, this method is a bit easier to master because it allows for greater speed and pressure.

Materials Needed:

- A bow (a curved stick with a cord tied to both ends)
- A straight stick (spindle)
- A flat piece of wood (fireboard)
- A socket (a small, hard piece of wood or rock to hold the spindle)
- Dry tinder

Steps:

- **Prepare the Fireboard:** Just like the hand drill method, carve a notch and a depression in the fireboard.
- **Set Up the Spindle:** Place the spindle in the bowstring loop and position it in the fireboard's depression.
- **Use the Bow:** Hold the bow with one hand and the socket with the other. Move the bow back and forth quickly, causing the spindle to spin.
- **Create an Ember:** As with the hand drill, keep going until you see smoke and an ember forms.
- **Transfer the Ember:** Carefully move the ember to your tinder and blow gently to start the fire.

Safety Tip: This method also requires adult supervision. Ensure that the area is safe for practicing fire making.

Flint and Steel

Using flint and steel is one of the easiest primitive fire-starting methods for kids to learn.

Materials Needed:

- A piece of flint or hard rock
- A steel striker (or any steel object with a sharp edge)
- Char cloth or dry tinder

Steps:

- **Hold the Flint:** Hold the flint in one hand and the steel in the other.
- **Strike the Steel:** Strike the steel against the flint at a sharp angle. This action creates sparks.
- **Catch the Spark:** Direct the sparks onto the char cloth or dry tinder.
- **Blow Gently:** Once the tinder catches a spark, blow gently to ignite it.

Safety Tip: Make sure to practice in a safe environment, and keep water nearby to control the fire.

Fire Plough

The fire plough is another friction-based method that is straightforward and engaging for young learners.

Materials Needed:

- A straight, dry stick (plough)
- A dry piece of wood (base)
- Dry tinder

Steps:

- **Prepare the Base:** Create a groove down the length of the wooden base.
- **Plough the Stick:** Rub the stick back and forth along the groove, applying pressure. This will generate heat and eventually an ember.
- **Transfer the Ember:** Once the ember forms, carefully move it to your tinder.
- **Blow Gently:** Blow softly to ignite the tinder.

Safety Tip: This method requires patience, so it's important to stay calm and focused. Always have an adult nearby.

Magnifying Glass (Solar Fire)

Using the sun to start a fire is simple and fascinating for kids.

Materials Needed:

- A magnifying glass
- Dry tinder

Steps:

- **Find a Sunny Spot:** On a sunny day, position yourself where the sun is strong.
- **Focus the Sunlight:** Hold the magnifying glass above the tinder. Adjust the angle until the sunlight focuses into a small, bright dot on the tinder.
- **Watch It Smoke:** Hold steady as the tinder begins to smoke and eventually catch fire.
- **Blow Gently:** Once it starts smoking, blow gently to encourage the flame.

Safety Tip: Never look directly at the sun and be sure to practice this method in a safe, open area.

> **Final Tips:**
> - Practice Makes Perfect: Primitive fire-making takes time to learn. Don't get discouraged if it doesn't work right away.
> - Always Be Safe: Never start a fire without permission and adult supervision.
> - Make sure you're in a safe place where a fire won't spread.
> - Respect the Fire: Fire is a powerful tool, but it can be dangerous. Always treat it with respect and care.

Putting Skills To Practice Project: Fire Starters

Cotton Ball and Vaseline Fire Starters

These fire starters are super simple to make and work really well.

What You'll Need:

- Cotton balls
- Vaseline (petroleum jelly)
- A small container or plastic bag for storage

How to Make Them:

1. Take a cotton ball and dip it into a glob of Vaseline.
2. Rub the Vaseline into the cotton ball until it's well-coated but not dripping.
3. Store your Vaseline-coated cotton balls in a small container or plastic bag until you're ready to use them.

How They Work:

- The cotton ball catches a spark or flame easily, and the Vaseline helps it burn longer. When you need to start a fire, just pull apart the cotton a little to expose the fibers, light it, and watch it burn!

Dryer Lint and Egg Carton Fire Starters

Don't throw away your dryer lint! It makes a great fire starter when combined with an old egg carton.

What You'll Need:

- Dryer lint
- An empty cardboard egg carton (not the styrofoam kind)
- Wax (old candle stubs work great)
- A pot for melting the wax (with adult supervision)

How to Make Them:

1. Stuff each section of the egg carton with dryer lint.

2. With an adult's help, melt some wax in a pot.

3. Carefully pour the melted wax over the dryer lint in each egg carton section.

4. Let the wax cool and harden. Then, cut the egg carton into individual sections so each piece is a fire starter.

How They Work:

- The dryer lint lights up easily, and the wax helps it burn longer, giving your fire a good start.

Toilet Paper Roll and Paper Towel Fire Starters

These fire starters are great for recycling and easy to make.

What You'll Need:

- Empty toilet paper rolls
- Paper towel or newspaper
- String or twine (optional)

How to Make Them:

1. Tear or cut the paper towel or newspaper into strips.

2. Roll up the strips of paper and stuff them tightly into the toilet paper roll.

3. If you want, you can tie a piece of string or twine around the middle to keep it all together, but it's not necessary.

How They Work:

- The paper inside the roll catches fire quickly, and the cardboard tube helps it burn longer, making it easier to start your fire.

Pinecone Fire Starters

What You'll Need:

- Pinecones (dry and clean)
- Wax (old candles or crayons work great)
- A pot for melting the wax (with adult supervision)
- String (optional)

How to Make Them:

1. With an adult's help, melt the wax in a pot.
2. Dip each pinecone into the melted wax, making sure it's well-coated.
3. If you want, tie a string around the top of the pinecone before dipping it, so you can hang it up to dry.
4. Let the wax harden on the pinecones, and then they're ready to use.

How They Work:

- The pinecone catches fire easily, and the wax makes it burn longer.
- They also look cool and can be used as decoration until you're ready to use them! How to Use Your Fire Starters:

How to Use Your Fire Starters:

When you're ready to start a fire, place your fire starter in the middle of your fire pit and surround it with kindling (small sticks or twigs). Light the fire starter, and it will help the kindling catch fire, making it easier to build your fire.

Making your own fire starters is fun and a great way to be prepared for your next camping trip or survival adventure. Plus, it's a cool way to recycle and use things you might already have around the house!

Using Matches and Lighters Safely

In survival situations, knowing how to safely use matches and lighters is an essential skill.

Basic Safety Rules for Using Matches and Lighters

1. **Keep Away from Young Children:** Matches and lighters should never be left where younger kids can reach them. Fire-starting tools can be dangerous if used improperly.
2. **Use Under Adult Supervision:** Always have an adult with you when using matches or lighters. They can help you stay safe and teach you the correct way to use these tools.
3. **Store Properly:** Matches and lighters should be kept in a waterproof container to protect them from rain and moisture. This keeps them ready to use when you need them.

How to Strike a Match Safely

1. **Hold the Match Correctly:** Hold the match at a slight angle with the head facing away from you. This helps ensure a safer strike.
2. **Strike Away from Your Body:** Strike the match head against the side of the matchbox or striker strip with a firm, quick motion. Make sure the match is away from your body to prevent burns.
3. **Shield from Wind:** Use your hand or body to shield the match from the wind. This helps the match light more easily and keeps the flame steady.

Types of Lighters and Their Uses

1. **Disposable Lighters:** These are easy to use and great for quick lighting. They usually have limited fuel, so they might need replacing after a while.

2. **Refillable Lighters:** These lighters can be refilled with fuel, making them more durable and long-lasting. They are a good choice for long-term use.

3. **Windproof Lighters:** These lighters are designed to work in windy conditions, which is useful if you're trying to start a fire outside in challenging weather.

Tips for Maintaining and Troubleshooting Lighters

1. **Refilling Butane Lighters:** If you have a refillable butane lighter, make sure to refill it with the proper butane fuel when it starts to run low.

2. **Checking and Replacing Flints:** If your lighter isn't working, it might need a new flint. Check the flint and replace it if necessary to keep the spark strong.

3. **Cleaning the Nozzle:** Keep the nozzle of your lighter clean to ensure a strong, consistent flame. Use a small brush or cloth to remove any dirt or residue.

Safety First!

Follow these safety tips and techniques to keep yourself and others safe.

- Always use matches and lighters with care.
- Remember that fire can be both useful and dangerous. Always handle it responsibly and never leave a lit match or lighter unattended.

By following these guidelines, you can learn to use matches and lighters safely and effectively, making your survival skills even stronger.

What Is a Rocket Stove and How Does It Work?

A rocket stove is a special kind of stove that burns wood very efficiently, meaning it uses less fuel and produces less smoke than a regular campfire. It's called a "rocket" stove because the way the air flows through it makes the fire burn hotter and faster, almost like a rocket!

How It Works:

- **Design:** The rocket stove has a tall, narrow chimney (a tube) where the fire burns. There's also a smaller tube at the bottom where you put the wood (fuel).

- **Airflow:** When you light the fire, air is pulled in through the bottom tube, which feeds the fire and makes it burn hotter. The hot air and smoke go up through the chimney, and since the stove is well-insulated, the heat is concentrated, making it more powerful.

- **Efficiency:** Because the rocket stove burns so hot, it uses less wood, and the wood burns completely, leaving very little ash or smoke. This makes it a great choice for cooking or boiling water in the wilderness or even in emergencies at home.

Now that you know what a rocket stove is and how it works, let's build one using simple and cheap supplies!

How to Build a Rocket Stove Out of an Aluminum Can

What You'll Need:

- A large aluminum can (like a coffee can)

- A smaller aluminum can (like a soup or vegetable can)

- Tin snips or heavy-duty scissors (for cutting the cans)

- A marker

- A pair of work gloves (to protect your hands)

- Sand or small rocks (optional, for insulation)

- A small piece of metal mesh or a few nails (for the grate)

Step 1: Prepare the Large Can

What to Do:

1. Take the large aluminum can and place it upside down (with the open end facing down).
2. Using the smaller can as a guide, trace a circle on the side of the large can near the bottom.

Why It's Important:

- This hole will be the opening where you'll feed the wood into the stove.

Step 2: Cut the Feed Tube Opening

What to Do:

1. Carefully use tin snips or heavy-duty scissors to cut out the circle you traced on the large can.
2. After cutting the hole, you can smooth the edges with sandpaper or bend them inward to avoid sharp edges.

Why It's Important:

- This hole needs to be big enough for the smaller can to fit through snugly, as it will become the feed tube for the wood.

Step 3: Prepare the Smaller Can

What to Do:

1. Take the smaller can and remove both the top and bottom lids.
2. Next, cut a hole in the side of the smaller can near one end, big enough for the wood to fit through.

Why It's Important:

- The smaller can will become the feed tube where you insert the sticks or wood, and the hole you cut will allow the wood to burn effectively.

Step 4: Assemble the Rocket Stove

What to Do:

1. Insert the smaller can into the hole you cut in the larger can. The hole in the smaller can should be facing upward inside the larger can.
2. If you want to insulate the stove (to make it more efficient), you can fill the space around the smaller can inside the larger can with sand or small rocks.

Why It's Important:

- The smaller can guides the airflow and wood into the fire, while the insulation helps keep the heat inside the stove, making it burn hotter and more efficiently.

Step 5: Add a Grate (Optional)

What to Do:

1. Place a small piece of metal mesh or lay a few nails across the top of the smaller can inside the large can.
2. This will act as a grate to hold the wood off the bottom of the can, allowing air to flow underneath the fire.

Why It's Important:

- The grate helps improve airflow, which is key to making the rocket stove work efficiently.

Step 6: Test Your Rocket Stove

What to Do:

1. Place small sticks or kindling into the smaller can (the feed tube).
2. Light the kindling and watch as the fire quickly heats up.
3. Once the fire is burning well, you can add more sticks or small pieces of wood to keep it going.

Why It's Important:

Testing your rocket stove helps you understand how to control the fire and keep it burning efficiently.

How It Works:

- **Feed Tube:** The smaller can feeds the wood into the fire and allows air to flow in, making the fire burn hotter.
- **Chimney Effect**: The large can acts as a chimney, directing heat upward and concentrating it, which is great for cooking.
- **Efficiency:** By using small sticks and kindling, the rocket stove creates a hot, clean-burning fire that uses less wood and produces less smoke.

Building your own rocket stove is a fun and useful project. It's a great way to learn about how fire works and how to cook or boil water in a survival situation. Plus, it's made from materials you can often find around the house, making it an easy and cheap way to be prepared!

Quiz:

Chapter 3 Fire: A Multipurpose Survival Tool

1. Why is fire important in a survival situation?

a) It keeps you entertained
b) It helps you stay warm, cook food, purify water, and signal for help
c) It scares away animals
d) It dries your clothes

2. Which of the following materials is considered tinder?

a) Large logs
b) Dry leaves or grass
c) Wet wood
d) Rocks

3. What shape is recommended for building a fire structure?

a) Square
b) Circle
c) Teepee
d) Pyramid

4. What should you do if your fire starts to die down?

a) Ignore it and hope it comes back
b) Pour water on it
c) Add more fuel and blow gently at the base
d) Throw sand on it

5. Which of these is NOT a primitive fire-starting method?

a) Hand Drill
b) Bow Drill
c) Flint and Steel
d) Electric lighter

6. What is the first step in building a fire?

a) Lighting the fire
b) Gathering kindling
c) Finding a safe spot
d) Adding fuel

7. How do you safely extinguish a fire?

a) Let it burn out on its own
b) Cover it with leaves
c) Pour water over it until the embers are out and the ashes are cool to the touch
d) Throw dirt on it and walk away

8. Which of these materials is used to make a fire starter?

a) Wet leaves
b) Pinecones and wax
c) Plastic bottles
d) Aluminum foil

9. What is a rocket stove designed to do?

a) Launch rockets
b) Burn wood very efficiently with less fuel and smoke
c) Make fire with no smoke
d) Cook food without any fuel

10. What safety tip is essential when using matches or lighters?

a) Use them indoors only
b) Strike the match away from your body
c) Always leave them unattended
d) Store them in a sunny spot

True or False

1. Tinder is used to keep a fire burning for a long time. (True/False)

2. Blowing gently at the base of a fire helps it burn stronger by providing more oxygen. (True/False)

3. The Bow Drill method is easier to master than the Hand Drill method because it allows for greater speed and pressure. (True/False)

4. A magnifying glass can be used to start a fire using the sun's rays. (True/False)

5. It's okay to leave a fire unattended if it's not very big. (True/False)

Short Answer Questions

1. What are the three main materials needed to start a fire, and why is each important?

2. Describe the steps to safely extinguish a fire.

3. Explain how a rocket stove works and why it's efficient.

4. Name one method of starting a fire without matches or a lighter and describe how it works.

5. What should you always do before leaving a fire site?

Chapter 4
Foraging

Foraging is like a treasure hunt in nature! You can find delicious and nutritious food growing all around you. Foraging means searching for wild plants that are safe to eat. It's a fun way to explore the outdoors and learn about the environment. But remember, not all wild plants are safe to eat, so it's important to learn how to identify the right ones.

Foraging Safety Rules

- **Always Have an Adult with You:** Foraging should be done with someone who knows which plants are safe and which are not.

- **Learn to Identify Plants:** Use a guidebook or an app to help you identify plants. Some plants look similar but can be very different—some are even poisonous.

- **Only Eat What You Know:** Never eat a plant unless you are 100% sure it's safe.

- **Respect Nature:** Only take what you need and leave enough for animals and other foragers.

- **Stay Away from Polluted Areas:** Don't forage near roads, industrial areas, or places where chemicals might have been used.

How to Start Foraging

Learn About Your Local Area: Start by learning which edible plants grow in your area. You can find books or online guides specific to your region.

- **Start with the Easy Ones:** Begin with plants that are easy to identify, like dandelions or blackberries.
- **Go on a Foraging Walk:** Take a walk with an experienced forager to learn in person.
- **Practice Plant Identification:** Even if you don't pick anything, practice identifying plants so you'll recognize them in the future.

Respect nature, take only what you need and never remove a whole plant if the entire thing is not going to be used for food or herbal remedies.

How to Identify Plants by Their Shapes, Colors, and Textures

Learning to identify plants is like solving a mystery in nature! To get started, you'll need to know how to look at a plant's shape, color, and texture.

1. Shapes of Plant Parts

Leaves:

- **Simple Leaves:** Single leaf on a stem, like a maple leaf.
- **Compound Leaves:** Multiple leaflets on one stem, like a clover.
- **Toothed Edges:** Leaves with jagged or serrated edges, like dandelions.
- **Smooth Edges:** Leaves with smooth, even edges, like a lilac.

Flowers:

- **Single Flower:** One flower per stem, like a daisy.
- **Clustered Flowers:** Many flowers grouped together, like a wildflower bouquet.
- **Spike:** Flowers arranged on a tall spike, like a foxglove.

Fruits:

- **Berries:** Small, round, and juicy, like blueberries.
- **Pods:** Long and skinny, like green beans.
- **Nuts:** Hard shell with a seed inside, like acorns.

Stems and Stalks:

- **Straight Stems:** Simple, straight stems like those of a sunflower.
- **Woody Stems:** Hard and sturdy, like a tree branch.
- **Flexible Stems:** Bendable and soft, like a grass stalk.

2. Colors of Plant Parts

Leaves:

- **Green:** Most leaves are green, but shades can vary from light to dark green.
- **Red or Purple:** Some plants have reddish or purplish leaves, like certain types of kale.

Flowers:

- **Bright Colors:** Flowers can be red, yellow, pink, blue, or purple. For example, violets are purple, and sunflowers are yellow.
- **White:** Some flowers are white, like daisies.

Fruits:

- **Colorful Fruits:** Fruits can be red (strawberries), blue (blueberries), or orange (wild oranges).

Stems:

- **Green:** Many stems are green, but some might be red or brown.

3. Textures of Plant Parts

Leaves:

- **Smooth:** Leaves that feel smooth to the touch, like a rose leaf.
- **Rough:** Leaves with a bumpy or hairy surface, like a lamb's ear.
- **Waxy:** Leaves with a shiny, waxy surface, like a holly leaf.

Flowers:

- **Soft Petals:** Flowers with soft and delicate petals, like a daisy.
- **Textured Petals:** Flowers with ridges or bumps, like a sunburst marigold.

Fruits:

- **Smooth Skin:** Fruits like apples have a smooth surface.
- **Bumpy Skin:** Fruits like blackberries have a bumpy texture.

Stems and Stalks:

- **Soft Stems:** Stems that are soft and flexible, like those of a grass plant.
- **Hard Stems:** Stems that are stiff and tough, like bamboo.

Recognizing and Foraging Edible Plants

Foraging for edible plants can be an exciting adventure, but it's important to learn how to recognize safe plants and avoid harmful ones and to use the Universal Edibility Test.

Key Characteristics of Edible Plants

Leaves:

- **Shape and Color:** Edible leaves can vary in shape and color. Look for leaves that are vibrant green and have a smooth or slightly toothed edge. Examples include dandelion and plantain.
- **Texture:** Some edible leaves are soft and tender, while others might be tougher and need cooking.

Flowers:

- **Color and Shape:** Many edible flowers are bright and colorful, like violets and dandelions. Check if the flower is listed as edible in guides.
- **Fragrance:** Edible flowers often have a pleasant smell, but make sure you can positively identify them.

Fruits:

- **Color and Size:** Edible fruits like wild strawberries or mulberries are small and colorful. They should be ripe but not overly squishy.

- **Taste:** Edible fruits should taste sweet or mildly tart. Be sure you know the fruit is safe before tasting.

Using Field Guides and Identification Apps

1. **Field Guides:**

- **Features:** Use books with clear pictures and descriptions of edible plants in your area. Look for guides specific to your region.

- **Practice:** Learn to compare the plants you find with the images and descriptions in the guide.

2. **Identification Apps:**

- **Features:** Apps can help you identify plants by uploading pictures or using the app's database.

- **Accuracy:** Use apps as a supplement to field guides and always double-check with multiple sources.

The Importance of Foraging Only Known Plants

- **Safety First:** Only eat plants you are 100% sure are safe. Even familiar-looking plants can sometimes be poisonous if misidentified.

- **Research:** Take time to learn and practice plant identification to avoid mistakes.

Universal Edibility Test

The Universal Edibility Test is a way to test unknown plants for safety. Here's how to do it:

1. **Separate the Plant into Parts:**

- Leaves, Stems, Roots, Buds, Flowers: Test each part of the plant separately.

2. **Test for Skin Reactions:**

- **Place on Skin:** Rub a small amount of the plant part on the inside of your wrist or elbow.

- **Wait:** Wait for 24 hours to check for any rash, redness, or irritation.

3. **Taste Test:**

- **Chew a Small Piece:** Chew a small part of the plant but don't swallow.

- **Wait:** Wait for 3 hours to see if there's any adverse reaction like nausea or itching before swallowing.

Common Toxic Plants to Avoid

1. **Poison Ivy, Oak, and Sumac:**

- **Identifying Features:** These plants often have shiny, red, or green leaves with a distinctive pattern (e.g., "leaves of three" for poison ivy).

- **Symptoms of Contact:** Itching, redness, and swelling after touching.

2. **Deadly Nightshade, Hemlock, and Foxglove:**

- **Recognizing Toxic Plants:**
  - **Deadly Nightshade:** Dark purple berries and bell-shaped flowers.
  - **Hemlock:** White, lacy flowers and fern-like leaves.
  - **Foxglove:** Tall spikes of tubular flowers, often in shades of purple.

- **Symptoms**: Severe symptoms include nausea, vomiting, and even death.

3. **Avoid Plants with Milky Sap or Bitter Taste:**

  - **Milky Sap:** Plants with white, milky sap can be toxic. Examples include milkweed.
  - **Bitter Taste:** Many toxic plants taste very bitter, which can be a warning sign.

15 Most Common Edible Plants in the United States

1. **Dandelion (Taraxacum officinale)**
   - **Edible Parts:** Leaves, flowers, and roots.
   - **Uses:** Leaves can be eaten raw in salads or cooked. Roots can be roasted for a coffee substitute.
   - **Medicinal Value:** Dandelion is a natural diuretic and helps with digestion.

2. **Wild Strawberries (Fragaria vesca)**
   - **Edible Parts:** Fruit.
   - **Uses:** Eat fresh or use in jams.
   - **Medicinal Value:** High in vitamin C, good for boosting the immune system.

3. **Chickweed (Stellaria media)**
   - **Edible Parts:** Leaves and stems.
   - **Uses:** Eat raw in salads or cook like spinach.
   - **Medicinal Value:** Can be used as a poultice for minor cuts and rashes.

4. **Cattail (Typha spp.)**
   - **Edible Parts:** Young shoots, flower spikes, and roots.
   - **Uses:** Shoots can be eaten like asparagus and roots can be ground into flour.
   - **Medicinal Value:** Cattail fluff can be used to dress wounds.

5. **Purslane (Portulaca oleracea)**
   - **Edible Parts:** Leaves and stems.
   - **Uses:** Eat raw in salads or cook as a vegetable.
   - **Medicinal Value:** High in omega-3 fatty acids, good for heart health.

6. **Lamb's Quarters (Chenopodium album)**
   - **Edible Parts:** Leaves.
   - **Uses:** Cook like spinach or eat raw in salads.
   - **Medicinal Value:** Rich in vitamins and minerals.

7. **Plantain (Plantago major)**
   - **Edible Parts:** Leaves.
   - **Uses:** Eat young leaves raw or cook like spinach.
   - **Medicinal Value:** Excellent for soothing insect bites and minor skin irritations.

8. **Wild Garlic (Allium vineale)**
    - **Edible Parts:** Leaves and bulbs.
    - **Uses:** Use like regular garlic in cooking.
    - **Medicinal Value:** Natural antibiotic properties, boosts immune system.

9. **Wild Onion (Allium canadense)**
    - **Edible Parts:** Leaves and bulbs.
    - **Uses:** Use in place of cultivated onions.
    - **Medicinal Value:** Supports heart health and fights colds.

10. **Wood Sorrel (Oxalis spp.)**
    - **Edible Parts:** Leaves, flowers, and seed pods.
    - **Uses:** Leaves have a lemony flavor, great in salads.
    - **Medicinal Value:** Helps with digestion and fevers.

11. **Violets (Viola spp.)**
    - **Edible Parts:** Leaves and flowers.
    - **Uses:** Flowers can be used in salads or as a garnish, leaves can be cooked like spinach.
    - **Medicinal Value:** Rich in vitamins A and C.

12. **Mulberries (Morus spp.)**
    - **Edible Parts:** Fruit.
    - **Uses:** Eat fresh, dry for snacks, or use in desserts.
    - **Medicinal Value:** Good source of antioxidants, supports immune health.

13. **Acorns (Quercus spp.)**
    - **Edible Parts:** Nuts.
    - **Uses:** Must be processed (leached to remove tannins) before eating, then used as flour or cooked.
    - **Medicinal Value:** Rich in nutrients, used in traditional medicine for treating skin issues.

14. **Red Clover (Trifolium pratense)**
    - **Edible Parts:** Flowers and leaves.
    - **Uses:** Flowers can be eaten raw or steeped as tea, leaves can be added to salads.
    - **Medicinal Value:** Used in herbal medicine for respiratory issues and as a blood purifier.

15. **Yarrow (Achillea millefolium)**
    - **Edible Parts:** Leaves and flowers.
    - **Uses:** Leaves can be used in salads or brewed as tea.
    - **Medicinal Value:** Known for its ability to stop bleeding, soothe colds, and reduce fevers.

A Fun and Tasty Survival Skill

Foraging is a fantastic way to learn survival skills, connect with nature, and find delicious food growing wild in the woods, fields, or even your own backyard! It really is like going on a treasure hunt where the prize is yummy, fresh food that you picked yourself. But while foraging can be fun and rewarding, it's important to remember that just because something is natural doesn't mean it's always safe to eat.

Why Being Careful Matters

Some wild plants, berries, and roots can cause allergic reactions in people. Even if a plant is safe for most people, it might cause a reaction in someone who is sensitive or allergic. Allergic reactions can range from mild, like a rash or upset stomach, to serious and potentially life-threatening problems, like difficulty breathing. That's why it's super important to be careful when you're trying new foods from the wild.

Foraging Safely: Important Tips

Check with Your Doctor: If you're taking any medications—even over-the-counter ones—or if you have any health conditions, talk to your doctor before eating wild plants. Some medicines can make you more likely to have a reaction to certain foods, even ones that are safe for most people.

Know Your Allergies: If you already have food allergies, make sure you're extra careful. Some wild plants might be related to foods you're allergic to and eating them could cause a reaction.

Be Aware of Medical Conditions: Certain medical conditions can make you more sensitive to wild foods. For example, people with hay fever might be more likely to react to plants like wild greens.

Informed Foraging Is Safe Foraging

Foraging is a wonderful and delicious skill that can help you survive in the wild. But it's also important to be smart and safe. The best way to enjoy foraging is by following the basics:

Remember, **"Informed Foraging Is Safe Foraging"** is a great motto to live by when you're out in the woods or fields looking for food. By being careful and knowledgeable, you can enjoy all the tasty rewards that foraging has to offer while staying safe.

Foraged Wild Food Simple Recipes

Dandelion Leaf Salad

Ingredients:

- Fresh dandelion leaves
- Wild garlic (optional)
- A splash of vinegar or lemon juice (if available)
- A pinch of salt (if available)

Instructions:

1. **Gather Dandelion Leaves:** Pick a handful of young dandelion leaves. Avoid older, tougher leaves.
2. **Wash the Leaves:** Rinse the leaves with clean water.
3. **Add Flavor (Optional):** If you have wild garlic, chop a small amount and mix it with the dandelion leaves.
4. **Season:** Add a splash of vinegar or lemon juice, and a pinch of salt if you have it.
5. **Mix and Eat:** Toss everything together and enjoy a fresh, crunchy salad!

> **Why It Works:** Dandelion leaves are packed with vitamins and have a slightly bitter but tasty flavor. Wild garlic adds a nice zing if available.

Wild Strawberry and Nut Mix

Ingredients:

- Fresh wild strawberries
- Nuts (if foraging for nuts, like acorns or walnuts, is an option)

Instructions:

1. **Pick Wild Strawberries:** Collect a handful of ripe wild strawberries.
2. **Gather Nuts:** If you can find and gather nuts, crush them into small pieces.
3. **Combine:** Mix the wild strawberries with the crushed nuts.
4. **Enjoy:** Eat this mixture as a sweet and nutty treat.

> **Why It Works:** Wild strawberries are sweet and nutritious, while nuts add a crunchy texture and extra energy.

Chickweed Pesto

Ingredients:

- Fresh chickweed leaves and stems
- A small amount of wild garlic (if available)
- Olive oil or any available oil (if not available, use water)
- Salt (if available)

Instructions:

1. **Pick Chickweed:** Collect a handful of chickweed leaves and stems.
2. **Chop Wild Garlic:** If you have wild garlic, chop it finely.
3. **Blend Ingredients:** If you have a blender or food processor, blend chickweed leaves and wild garlic with a little oil or water until smooth. Add salt if available.
4. **Serve:** Use the pesto as a dip for other wild foods or spread it on bread if you have it.

> **Why It Works:** Chickweed is mild and nutritious, and wild garlic adds flavor to the pesto.

Cattail Shoot Wraps

Ingredients:

- Fresh cattail shoots
- Edible wild leaves (like dandelion or plantain leaves)

Instructions:

1. **Harvest Cattail Shoots:** Collect young, tender cattail shoots.
2. **Prepare Leaves:** Pick some edible wild leaves like dandelion or plantain.
3. **Wrap Shoots:** Place the cattail shoots inside the wild leaves and roll them up.
4. **Eat:** Enjoy these wraps as a crunchy, green snack.

> **Why It Works:** Cattail shoots are tender and mild, while wild leaves add flavor and make the wraps easy to handle.

Wood Sorrel Lemonade

Ingredients:

- Fresh wood sorrel leaves
- Water

Instructions:

1. **Gather Wood Sorrel:** Collect a handful of wood sorrel leaves.
2. **Prepare Water:** If you have access to clean water, pour some into a container.
3. **Steep Leaves:** Add the wood sorrel leaves to the water and let them steep for a few minutes. The wood sorrel will give the water a tangy flavor.
4. **Strain and Drink:** Remove the leaves and drink the tangy, refreshing water.

> **Why It Works:** Wood sorrel has a natural lemony flavor that makes a refreshing drink. It's also rich in vitamin C. This vitamin is important for your general health and immune system.

Safe Foraging in Urban Areas

Urban foraging is the practice of finding and harvesting edible plants and food sources in cities. Even though cities might seem like a concrete jungle, many edible plants and food sources can be found in urban environments. It's a way to connect with nature, save money, and enjoy fresh, healthy food. But it's important to be smart and safe while foraging in urban areas!

Identifying Safe Urban Foraging Spots

Here's how to find good places to forage in the city:

1. **Community Gardens and Public Parks:**
   - Community gardens are great because they are often well-maintained and have a variety of edible plants.
   - Public parks might have wild plants and fruits, especially in less-tended areas.

2. **Abandoned Lots with Wild Plants:**
   - Sometimes, abandoned lots can be full of wild edibles like dandelions and clover.
   - Make sure these areas aren't contaminated and avoid foraging near litter or pollution.

3. **Edible Landscapes:**
   - Many cities have fruit trees and berry bushes planted in public spaces.
   - Look for apple trees, cherry trees, and berry bushes in parks or along sidewalks.

Common Urban Edible Plants

Here are some edible plants you might find in urban areas:

1. **Dandelions (Taraxacum officinale):**
   - **Where to Find:** Lawns, parks, and garden beds.
   - **Edible Parts:** Leaves, flowers, and roots.
   - **How to Use:** Leaves can be eaten raw or cooked; flowers can be used in salads; roots can be roasted.

2. **Clover (Trifolium spp.):**
   - **Where to Find:** Lawns, parks, and grassy areas.
   - **Edible Parts:** Leaves and flowers.
   - **How to Use:** Leaves can be eaten raw in salads; flowers can be used as a garnish.

3. **Plantain (Plantago major):**
   - **Where to Find:** Lawns, sidewalks, and neglected areas.
   - **Edible Parts:** Leaves.
   - **How to Use:** Eat young leaves raw or cook like spinach.

4. **Fruit Trees:**
   - **Where to Find:** Community gardens, public parks, and urban green spaces.
   - **Types:** Apples, cherries, pears.
   - **How to Use:** Eat fresh or use in recipes like pies or jams.

5. **Berry Bushes:**
   - **Where to Find:** Public spaces and urban gardens.
   - **Types:** Raspberries, blackberries, and blueberries.
   - **How to Use:** Eat fresh or use in smoothies and desserts.

6. **Herbs:**
   - Where to Find: Public spaces, community gardens.
   - Types: Mint, parsley, and chives.
   - How to Use: Use fresh in cooking or as a garnish.

Safety Tips for Urban Foraging

Avoid Contaminated Areas:

- Stay away from areas with heavy traffic or industrial pollution.
- Avoid foraging near litter, pet waste, or areas that might be contaminated.

Wash All Foraged Food Thoroughly:

- Always wash fruits, vegetables, and herbs thoroughly to remove any dirt or pollutants.
- Rinse with clean water and consider peeling or cooking the food to ensure safety.

Know Local Laws and Regulations:

- Check local regulations about foraging in public areas. Some places might have rules or restrictions on picking plants or fruits.
- Always follow the rules to avoid fines or legal issues.

Forage Responsibly:

- Only take what you need and leave enough for other foragers and wildlife.
- Be respectful of public spaces and avoid damaging plants or property.

Quiz:
Chapter 4 - Foraging

1. What is foraging?

a) Finding treasure in the woods
b) Searching for wild plants that are safe to eat
c) Collecting rocks and minerals
d) Hunting for animals

2. **True or False:** You should only eat a plant if you are 100% sure it is safe.

3. What should you do if you find a plant you don't recognize while foraging?

a) Eat it anyway to see if it's good
b) Ask an adult who knows about plants
c) Ignore it and keep walking
d) Pick it and take it home for later

4. **Match the plant parts with their description:**

- Leaves
    - Small, round, and juicy
- Flowers
    - Hard shell with a seed inside
- Fruits
    - Multiple leaflets on one stem
- Stems
    - Simple, straight stems

5. **True or False:** You should forage near roads and industrial areas because plants there are often the safest to eat.

6. What is the Universal Edibility Test used for?

a) To check if a plant is tasty
b) To see if a plant is safe to eat
c) To find out how old a plant is
d) To determine the plant's color

7. **Name one edible plant from the list in the chapter.**

8. **What should you do before eating any wild plant?**

a) Check if it looks interesting
b) Perform the Universal Edibility Test
c) Smell it to see if it smells good
d) Cook it and hope for the best

9. True or False: Poison Ivy, Oak, and Sumac are safe to touch and eat.

10. Why is it important to respect nature while foraging?

a) To avoid getting lost
b) To ensure you find the best plants
c) To leave enough for animals and other foragers and not harm the environment
d) To get a good workout

Chapter 5
Hunting, Fishing, and Simple Trapping Techniques

Hunting, fishing, and trapping have been essential skills practiced by humans for thousands of years as reliable methods for securing food. In this chapter, you'll explore key survival techniques that draw upon these time-honored practices.

Trapping is a great skill to learn for survival situations. It can provide a reliable source of protein and requires minimal effort once the traps are set. Understanding how to trap can help you stay well-fed and healthy if you're ever in a survival situation.

Materials Needed for Basic Traps

To build simple traps, you'll need a few basic materials that you can often find in nature or include in a survival kit:

- **Sticks and Vines:** These can be used to create the structure and noose of your trap.
- **Natural Cordage:** If you don't have vines, you can make cordage from plants like cattails or bark.
- **Sharp Stones or Knife:** Useful for cutting and shaping your materials.
- **Bait:** Food scraps, nuts, or fruits to attract the animal.

Here's how you can create a simple snare trap using natural materials:

Step-by-Step Instructions For Building A Simple Snare Trap

1. **Find a Game Trail:**
   - Look for animal tracks or paths where animals frequently travel. These trails are good places to set your trap.

2. **Create a Noose:**
   - Use natural cordage or vines to make a loop. The loop should be large enough for the animal to enter but small enough to tighten around its neck or body.
   - Tie the ends of the cordage together to form a loop. It should be adjustable so it can tighten as the animal moves through it.

3. **Set the Noose:**
   - Find a sturdy branch or stake. Tie one end of the noose to the branch or stake, leaving the loop hanging down in the game trail.
   - Make sure the loop is positioned at the right height and width to catch the animal.

4. **Secure the Trap:**
   - To keep the noose in place, you may need to anchor it with sticks or other materials.
   - Make sure the noose is free to move and tighten when an animal enters it.

5. **Use Bait:**
   - Place some bait, such as food scraps or nuts, near or inside the loop. The bait will attract the animal and encourage it to enter the noose.

Safety and Ethical Considerations for Trapping

When trapping, it's important to be responsible and respectful of animals and nature. Here are some key points to keep in mind:

- **Check Traps Regularly:**
  - Always check your traps frequently to ensure that animals do not suffer for long periods. This also helps you avoid catching non-target animals.

- **Ensure Humane Dispatch:**
  - If you catch an animal, it should be dispatched quickly and humanely to minimize suffering. Learn proper techniques for handling trapped animals.

Types of Small Game You Can Catch with a Simple Snare Trap

A simple snare trap is designed to catch small animals that are relatively easy to find and track. Here's some common small game you can catch with a snare trap, along with their signs and tracks to help you locate them.

1. **Rabbits**

- **Description:** Rabbits are small, furry animals with long ears and short tails. They often hide in grassy or bushy areas.
- **Signs and Tracks:**
  - **Tracks:** Look for small, rounded footprints with a distinct pattern of four toes. The tracks are usually about 2-3 inches long.
  - **Droppings:** Small, round pellets scattered around their habitat.
  - **Feeding Signs:** Chewed plants and leaves, especially at ground level.

2. **Squirrels**

- **Description:** Squirrels are small rodents with bushy tails. They are usually found in wooded areas and are excellent climbers.
- **Signs and Tracks:**
  - **Tracks:** Look for small, clawed footprints with five toes on the front paws and four on the back paws. Tracks are often about 1-2 inches long.
  - **Droppings:** Small, cylindrical droppings often found under trees or near their nests.
  - **Feeding Signs:** Shredded nuts, chewed tree bark, and scattered acorns.

3. **Possums (Opossums)**

- **Description:** Possums are larger than rabbits and squirrels, with a long, prehensile tail and a somewhat rat-like appearance.
- **Signs and Tracks:**
  - **Tracks:** Look for tracks with five toes on both the front and back feet, with the front tracks showing a thumb-like appendage.
  - **Droppings:** Irregular, sometimes segmented droppings.
  - **Feeding Signs:** Scattered food scraps, overturned leaves, and evidence of digging.

4. **Raccoons**

- **Description**: Raccoons have distinctive black **"mask"** markings around their eyes and a bushy tail with rings. They are common in wooded and semi-urban areas.

- **Signs and Tracks:**
  - **Tracks:** Look for tracks with five toes on both front and back feet, with the front feet having a somewhat hand-like appearance.
  - **Droppings:** Often found in latrine sites; they may be dark and contain undigested food.
  - **Feeding Signs:** Scattered food scraps, overturned objects, and disturbed soil.

5. Skunks

- **Description:** Skunks are recognizable by their distinctive black and white stripes. They are usually found in forested or grassy areas.
- **Signs and Tracks:**
  - **Tracks:** Look for tracks similar to those of raccoons, with five toes and a rounded shape. They often leave a distinctive odor behind.
  - **Droppings:** Dark and tubular, sometimes with a strong odor.
  - **Feeding Signs:** Disturbed soil, scattered food remains, and overturned debris.

Locating Small Game: Tips for Young Foragers

1. Look for Trails:

- Animals often follow the same paths. Look for worn trails through the grass or leaves.

2. Check Underbrush:

- Many small animals hide or nest in dense bushes or underbrush. Look carefully around these areas.

3. Listen and Observe:

- Pay attention to sounds like rustling leaves or scratching. Observing animal behavior can also help you find their homes.

4. Follow Animal Signs:

- Look for droppings, tracks, and feeding signs to determine which animals are in the area and where they might be traveling.

5. Be Quiet and Stealthy:

- Animals can be easily scared away. Move quietly and avoid sudden movements to increase your chances of spotting or catching them.

Putting Skills to Practice Project: PVC Bow for Small Game Hunting

Making your own bow out of PVC pipe is a fun and practical project that can be used for hunting small game or to hone your aim during target practice. PVC bows are durable, easy to make, and can be surprisingly effective if constructed correctly.

Materials Needed:

- 1-inch diameter PVC pipe (length will vary depending on your height)
- PVC pipe cutter or saw
- PVC pipe fittings (T-joints and elbow joints)
- Heat source (heat gun or stove)
- Strong cord or bowstring (such as Dacron string or heavy-duty nylon cord)
- Drill and drill bits
- Sandpaper or a file
- Measuring tape
- Marker or pencil

Step-by-Step Instructions

1. **Measure and Cut the PVC Pipe**

- **Determine Length:** Measure from the tip of one hand to the tip of the other hand when extended. This is approximately the length of your bow. A common length is between 4 to 5 feet.

- **Cut the Pipe:** Using a PVC pipe cutter or saw, cut two pieces of PVC pipe to this length. These will be the limbs of your bow.

2. **Shape the Bow**

- **Heat the PVC:** Carefully heat the PVC pipe using a heat gun or stove. Be cautious not to overheat as it can melt the pipe. The goal is to make it flexible enough to bend.

- **Bend the Pipe:** Once the pipe is heated and flexible, gently bend each piece into a curved shape. Make sure both pieces have a similar curve to ensure balanced performance.

- **Allow to Cool:** Hold the curved shape until the PVC cools and hardens. You can use clamps or braces to maintain the shape while cooling.

3. **Assemble the Bow**

- **Attach Fittings:** Use PVC fittings to connect the two limbs. Attach a T-joint to the ends of the limbs, then connect them using elbow joints to form the bow's handle. Ensure the fittings are securely glued or fitted.

- **Create the Handle:** Cut a short piece of PVC pipe to use as the bow's handle. Attach it to the center of the T-joint.

4. **Prepare the Bowstring**

- **Measure and Cut String:** Measure the length of your bow and cut the bowstring accordingly, allowing extra length for tying knots. A typical bowstring is slightly shorter than the length of the bow.

- **Attach the String:** Tie the bowstring securely to each end of the bow. You may need to drill small holes at the ends of the limbs to thread the string through. Make sure the string is taut but not overly tight.

5. **Test and Adjust**

- **Check Tension:** Draw the bowstring back to ensure it has the correct tension.

- Adjust as needed by tightening or loosening the string.

- **Test for Performance:** Use the bow for target practice to test how good it is. Adjust the shape or string tension if necessary to improve performance.

How and Why It Works:

- **PVC Flexibility:** PVC pipe is lightweight and flexible, making it an ideal material for a bow. The heat treatment allows it to be bent into a curved shape, which is essential for creating the bow's limbs.

- **String Tension:** The bowstring stores and transfers energy when drawn and released. The PVC limbs flex and store energy, which is then transferred to the arrow, propelling it forward.

- **Durability:** PVC is resistant to moisture and weathering, making it a durable choice for outdoor use.

> ### Tips for Using Your PVC Pipe Bow:
>
> - **Practice Regularly:** Like any bow, accuracy and skill come with practice. Spend time improving your aim and technique.
>
> - **Use Proper Arrows:** Ensure your arrows are suitable for your bow. They should be lightweight and have a proper fletching for stability.
>
> - **Maintain Your Bow:** Check the bowstring and limbs regularly for wear and tear. Replace or repair any damaged parts to ensure safe and effective use.
>
> - **Safety First:** Always use your bow in a safe area, away from people and animals. Follow all safety guidelines for shooting and handling.

Basic Fishing Skills

Fishing is a fantastic skill to learn, especially in a survival situation. It's an enjoyable activity that can provide a reliable and nutritious food source. Let's dive into the basics of fishing, including how to make your own gear, catch fish, and prepare them for a meal.

Why Fishing Is Important

1. **Abundance of Fish:** Many environments, like lakes, rivers, and streams, have plenty of fish. This means you have a good chance of catching something to eat.

2. **High Nutritional Value:** Fish are packed with protein and healthy fats, which are great for keeping you strong and energized.

Putting Skills to Practice: Making Simple Fishing Gear

Improvising a Fishing Rod:

- **Materials Needed:** A sturdy stick, string or vine.
- **Instructions:** Find a straight stick about as long as your arm. Tie one end of the string or vine to the tip of the stick. This will be your fishing rod.

Making Hooks:

- **Materials Needed:** Safety pins, bones, or thorns.
- **Instructions:** If using safety pins, straighten the pin and then bend it into a hook shape. If using bones or thorns, carefully shape them into a hook with a knife or sharp stone.

Using Natural Line:

- **Materials Needed:** Vines, shoelaces, or strong threads.
- **Instructions:** Cut a piece of vine or thread long enough to reach from your rod to the water. Tie it securely to your hook.

Basic Fishing Techniques

1. **Selecting a Fishing Spot:**
   - Look for calm areas of water where fish are likely to be. Places with plants or rocks are good because fish like to hide there.

2. **Baiting the Hook:**
   - **Materials:** Worms, insects, or food scraps.
   - **Instructions:** Thread the bait onto your hook so it is securely attached.

3. **Casting the Line:**
   - Hold your fishing rod with the baited hook over the water. Gently swing the rod forward to cast the line into the water. Let the bait sink and wait patiently.

4. **Setting the Hook:**
   - When you feel a tug on the line, quickly pull the rod up to set the hook in the fish's mouth.

5. **Reeling In the Fish:**
   - Gently pull the fish towards you by slowly and steadily reeling in the line.

Cleaning and Cooking Fish

Cleaning the Fish:

- **Removing Scales:** Use a knife or sharp stone to scrape off the fish scales, starting from the tail and moving towards the head.
- **Gutting:** Make a cut along the belly of the fish from the tail to the head. Remove the insides and discard them.

Cooking Methods:

- Grilling Over an Open Fire: Skewer the fish on a stick and hold it over the fire, turning occasionally until it is cooked through.
- **Using Hot Stones:** Place hot stones in a pit and lay the fish on top. Cover with more hot stones and let cook for a while.

Ensuring Thorough Cooking:

- Make sure the fish is cooked all the way through to avoid any parasites. The flesh should be opaque and flake easily with a fork.

Safety Tips

- **Handle the Fish Carefully:** Fish can be slippery, so use care when cleaning and cooking them.
- **Avoid Parasites:** Ensure the fish is fully cooked to kill any parasites that might be present.
- **Stay Safe Around Fire:** Always use fire safety precautions when cooking.

Quiz:

Chapter 5 Hunting, Fishing and Trapping

1. What materials are needed to build a basic snare trap?

   a) Only sticks and vines
   b) Sticks, vines, natural cordage, sharp stones or knife, and bait
   c) Only bait and a knife
   d) Only natural cordage and bait

2. When setting a snare trap, why is it important to place bait near the noose?

   a) To make the trap look pretty
   b) To attract the animal to the trap
   c) To hide the trap from the animal
   d) To make the trap easier to spot

3. What should you do if you catch an animal in a trap?

   a) Leave it in the trap until you come back later
   b) Dispatch it quickly and humanely
   c) Release it immediately without checking
   d) Take a picture and then release it

4. Which of the following is NOT a sign of a rabbit's presence?

   a) Small, rounded footprints
   b) Chewed plants and leaves
   c) Small, cylindrical droppings
   d) Chewed plants and leaves

5. How can you identify a raccoon's tracks?

   a) They have five toes and a somewhat hand-like appearance on the front feet
   b) They have a single, large paw print
   c) They are similar to a rabbit's tracks
   d) They are small and round with four toes

6. What is one way to make a simple fishing rod?

   a) Use a piece of string tied to a stick
   b) Use a fishing reel tied to a branch
   c) Use a vine tied to a tree
   a) Use a fishing line tied to a shoe

7. When fishing, what should you do if you feel a tug on the line?

   a) Pull the rod up quickly to set the hook
   b) Let the line go slack
   c) Immediately cast the line again
   d) Wait and see if the fish swims away

8. **What is a safe and effective way to cook fish?**

a) Boil it in water
b) Grill it over an open fire
c) Leave it in the sun to dry
d) Freeze it in cold water

9. **Which material is NOT recommended for making fishing hooks?**

a) Safety pins
b) Bones
c) Thorns
d) Plastic straws

10. **Why should you check your traps regularly?**

a) To avoid catching non-target animals
b) To see if the traps are still visible
c) To find out if the traps are in the right location
d) To see if the bait needs to be replaced

Chapter 6
Shelter

When you're out in the wilderness, finding or building a shelter is crucial for your safety and comfort. A good shelter protects you from wind, rain, and cold, helping you stay dry and warm. It also keeps you safe from wildlife and provides a place to rest. In emergencies, a shelter is a must-have to keep you both comfortable and safe.

Shelter: Your First Line of Defense

- **Protection from the Elements:** A good shelter protects you from wind, rain, snow, and sun, helping you maintain your body temperature.
- **Safety:** Shelter can also provide a safe space from wild animals and insects, keeping you secure during the night.
- **Rest:** A well-constructed shelter gives you a place to rest and recover your energy, which is essential for survival.

Why Shelter Is Important

Shelter is often the most urgent need in a survival situation, especially if you're exposed to extreme weather like freezing cold, scorching heat, or heavy rain. Without proper shelter, your body can quickly lose or gain too much heat, leading to dangerous conditions like hypothermia or heatstroke.

Types of Shelter

- **Natural Shelters:** These are made using what you find around you, like caves, large tree branches, or rock overhangs.
- **Man-Made Shelters:** If you have tools or materials, you can build a shelter using tarps, sticks, leaves, or even snow. The goal is to create a structure that keeps you dry, warm, and protected.

How to Gather Materials Safely

1. Find Long Branches: Look for branches that are long and strong. Make sure they are not brittle.
2. Collect Smaller Sticks and Leaves: Gather a variety of small sticks and leaves to use for covering the shelter.
3. Look for Natural Cordage: Find vines or roots that are strong enough to hold the branches together. If you don't have natural cordage, shoelaces can work too.

Building Your Lean-To Shelter: Step-by-Step

What is a Lean-To Shelter?

A lean-to shelter is a simple, effective structure that provides protection from the elements. It's called a "lean-to" because it leans against a sturdy support, like a tree or a rock. It's easy to build with natural materials and can be set up quickly.

Materials You Will Need:

- **Long, Sturdy Branches:** These will form the main frame of your shelter.
- **Smaller Sticks:** These are used to cover and insulate the shelter.
- **Leaves, Grass, or Pine Needles:** These materials help with insulation and waterproofing.
- **Natural Cordage:** You can use vines, roots, or even shoelaces to tie the branches together.

1. **Choose a Good Location:**
   - **Near Resources:** Set up your shelter near water and food sources.
   - **Away from Hazards:** Avoid areas with falling rocks, dead trees, or other dangers.

2. **Set Up the Frame:**
   - **Find a Support:** Use a tree or a large rock as the main support for your shelter.
   - **Lean Branches:** Place the long branches against the support at an angle, forming a slanted roof. Make sure they are stable and secure.

3. **Add Coverage:**
   - **Layer Sticks:** Place smaller sticks across the long branches, from bottom to top, to create a sturdy base.
   - **Insulate with Leaves:** Cover the sticks with leaves, grass, or pine needles. This will help keep the shelter warm and dry.
   - **Secure Everything:** Use your natural cordage or improvised ties to make sure everything stays in place.

4. **Check for Gaps:**
   - **Cover Openings:** Make sure there are no gaps where wind or rain can enter. Add more leaves or sticks if needed.

5. **Test It Out:**
   - **Ensure Comfort:** Sit inside your shelter to check for any areas that need improvement. Make sure it's dry and snug.

Tips to Build the Perfect Shelter

- **Stay Safe:** Always be cautious when gathering materials. Look out for sharp objects or dangerous plants.
- **Adapt as Needed:** You can adjust the size and shape of your shelter based on your needs and the materials available.
- **Practice Makes Perfect:** The more you practice building shelters, the better you'll become. Try building different types of shelters to learn more.

Improving and Maintaining Your Shelter

Once you've built your lean-to shelter, there are a few ways to make it even better and ensure it stays in great shape. Here's how you can enhance your shelter's comfort and durability:

Adding More Layers for Better Insulation

1. **Insulate with More Materials:**
   - **Layer Extra Leaves or Pine Needles:** Add more leaves, pine needles, or grass to the roof and walls of your shelter. This extra layer will help keep the warmth in and the cold out.
   - **Use Moss or Ferns:** If available, moss or ferns can also provide excellent insulation. Just be sure they're clean and dry before adding them.

2. **Seal Gaps:**
   - Patch Holes: If you find any gaps or holes, fill them in with extra materials. This will help prevent wind and rain from getting inside.

3. **Make it Weather-Resistant:**
   - **Add a Waterproof Layer:** If you expect rain, add a layer of large leaves or a tarp over the top of the shelter to keep water from soaking through.

Regularly Checking and Reinforcing the Structure

1. **Inspect the Shelter:**
   - **Look for Weak Spots:** Regularly check your shelter for any weak spots or areas that need repair. Look at the frame, the covering, and the tie points.
   - **Fix Damage Promptly:** If you notice any damage, fix it as soon as possible. Reinforce the structure by adding more sticks or securing loose branches.

2. **Reinforce the Frame:**
   - **Strengthen the Support:** If the main support branches start to lean or shift, reinforce them with additional sticks or by securing them with more cordage.
   - **Check Ties:** Make sure the natural cordage or shoelaces are still tight and holding everything in place. Replace or tighten them if needed.

Creating a Comfortable Bed

1. **Build a Bed of Leaves or Pine Needles:**
   - **Gather Soft Materials:** Collect a large pile of leaves, pine needles, or grass to create a soft, cushioned bed inside your shelter.
   - **Layer for Comfort:** Spread the materials evenly on the ground where you'll be sleeping. Add more layers for extra comfort.

2. **Elevate Your Sleeping Area:**
   - Create a Raised Platform: If possible, build a small platform using sticks or branches to keep your bedding off the cold, damp ground. This can help you stay warmer and drier.

3. **Add a Blanket or Sleeping Bag:**
   - Use Available Materials: If you have a blanket or sleeping bag, use it inside your shelter for added warmth and comfort.

Final Tips

- **Keep Your Shelter Clean:** Regularly remove any debris or dirt from inside the shelter to keep it comfortable and dry.
- **Adapt as Needed:** If the weather changes or you find new materials, adjust your shelter to improve its performance.
- **Practice and Learn:** The more you use and maintain your shelter, the better you'll become at making it comfortable and durable.

Constructing a Debris Hut

A debris hut is a fantastic type of shelter to build when you're out in the wilderness. It's especially useful in cold and wet conditions. Why? Because it provides excellent insulation from the cold and rain using materials you find in nature. Plus, it helps you stay hidden from view—great for staying stealthy and safe. It's also a good choice if you're on your own, as it's relatively simple to build.

Materials You Will Need:

To build a sturdy and warm debris hut, gather these materials:

- **Sturdy Branch (Ridgepole):** This is the main support for your hut. It should be strong and long enough to reach between two supports, like trees or rocks.
- **Leaves, Grass, and Small Branches (Debris):** These materials will form the insulation layer over your hut.
- **Supporting Sticks:** These help create the frame for your hut.

How to Gather Materials:

1. **Find a Sturdy Branch:** Look for a strong, straight branch that's long enough to serve as the ridgepole. This will be the top beam of your hut.

2. **Collect Debris:** Gather lots of leaves, grass, and small branches. These will go over the frame to keep you warm and dry.

3. **Find Supporting Sticks:** Look for smaller sticks that can be used to form the frame of your hut.

Step-by-Step Instructions

1. **Choose Your Site:**
    - Find a location with plenty of debris material nearby.
    - Pick a spot that's flat and away from any hazards like falling branches or rushing water.

2. **Place the Ridgepole:**
    - Position the ridgepole between two supports like trees or rocks.
    - Make sure it's securely balanced and won't fall over.

3. **Create the Frame:**
    - Lean smaller sticks against the ridgepole, forming a V-shape.
    - Arrange the sticks closely together to make a sturdy frame.

4. **Pile on the Debris:**
    - Start covering the frame with leaves, grass, and small branches.
    - Pile the debris thickly to create a good insulation layer that will keep you warm and dry.

Tips for Optimizing Your Debris Hut

- **Thick Insulation:** Make sure the debris layer is thick enough. The thicker it is, the better it will insulate you from the cold and rain.
- **Small Entrance:** Create a small entrance to help keep the heat inside. You can use additional debris to close it up when you're inside.
- **Comfortable Bedding:** Add extra debris inside the hut to make a bed. Use leaves or pine needles for extra warmth and comfort.

Making a Snow Shelter – Igloos and Quinzees

When winter hits, finding or creating a good shelter is key to staying warm and safe. Snow can be a fantastic material for building shelters that keep you cozy even when it's freezing outside. In this section, we'll explore how to make two types of snow shelters: igloos and quinzees.

Benefits of Snow Shelters

Snow shelters are amazing because of the following:

- **Warmth:** Snow is a natural insulator, which means it helps keep the heat from your body inside the shelter. Even when it's really cold outside, the inside of your snow shelter can stay warm.

- **Materials:** Snow is everywhere in winter, so it's a great resource for building shelters.

- **Protection:** Snow shelters shield you from harsh winds and snowstorms, making them a reliable option for survival in snowy conditions.

Tools and Materials Needed

For Building Igloos:

- Shovel or Improvised Digging Tools: You can use a shovel if you have one, or even sticks and your hands to dig and shape the snow.
- Snow Blocks: You'll need to cut and shape snow into blocks for building the igloo.

For Building Quinzees:

- Shovel or Improvised Digging Tools: As with igloos, you'll need tools to pack and shape the snow.
- Packed Snow: Instead of blocks, you'll use packed snow to build the quinzee.

Building an Igloo

1. **Finding the Right Spot:**

- Look for a flat area with deep, compact snow. Avoid places where snow might be too soft or where the ground could be uneven.

2. **Cutting and Shaping Snow Blocks:**

- Use a shovel or your hands to cut large blocks of snow. They should be about 12 inches (30 cm) wide and 6 inches (15 cm) high.

3. **Stacking Blocks:**

- Place the blocks in a spiral pattern, starting from the outside and working your way up to the center. Overlap the blocks slightly as you build upward to create a dome shape.

4. **Creating the Dome Shape:**

- As you stack the blocks, curve them inward to form a dome. This shape helps to keep the shelter stable and strong.

5. **Adding Ventilation Holes:**

- Make sure to carve small ventilation holes at the top of the igloo. This allows fresh air to flow in and prevents the shelter from getting too stuffy.

Building a Quinzee

1. **Piling Up Snow:**

- Pile snow into a large mound, about 6 to 8 feet (2 to 2.5 meters) high and wide. Make sure the mound is compacted well.

2. **Letting Snow Settle:**

- Allow the snow to settle and harden for several hours. This helps it hold its shape when you start hollowing it out.

3. **Hollowing Out the Mound:**

- Carefully dig into the mound from the top to create an interior space. Make sure to leave a thick layer of snow on all sides to keep the shelter insulated.

4. **Adding Ventilation Holes:**

- Carve a small ventilation hole in the top of the quinzee to let fresh air in.

5. **Smoothing the Interior Walls:**

- Smooth out the inside walls to make them more comfortable and to help prevent any ice formation.

Safety Considerations for Snow Shelters

Checking Stability:

- Regularly check that your shelter is stable and secure. If you notice any cracks or weak spots, reinforce them with more snow.

Ensuring Ventilation:

- Always make sure there is proper ventilation to be able to breathe properly. Ventilation holes should be open and unobstructed.

Avoiding Direct Contact with Snow:

- Create a bedding area using leaves, pine needles, or other materials to keep you from lying directly on the snow. This helps prevent heat loss and keeps you warmer.

Urban Shelter Solutions – Finding Safe Spots in the City

When you're in a city, finding shelter can be crucial during emergencies or unexpected situations. Whether it's due to a natural disaster, getting lost, or needing temporary refuge, knowing where and how to find safe spots in the urban environment can help you stay protected and secure.

Importance of Urban Shelters in Emergencies

In cities, shelters become essential in various situations:

- **Natural Disasters:** Events like earthquakes, storms, or floods can damage buildings and create unsafe conditions. Sheltering in a safe, sturdy location is crucial for your protection.

- **Getting Lost:** If you find yourself lost in the city, finding a safe place to stay can help you stay safe while waiting for help.

- **Temporary Displacement:** Sometimes, you may need a temporary place to stay due to unexpected situations like power outages or evacuations.

Identifying Common Safe Spots in Urban Areas

Knowing where to look for safe spots can make a big difference:

1. **Public Buildings:**
   - **Libraries, Schools, and Community Centers:** These places are often open to the public and can provide temporary shelter. Look for the nearest ones and head there if you need safety.

2. **Abandoned Structures:**
   - **With Caution:** Abandoned buildings can sometimes offer shelter, but be very careful. Make sure the structure is stable and safe to enter. Avoid places that look too dangerous or are in disrepair.

3. **Underpasses and Bridges:**
   - **Temporary Protection:** These can provide protection from rain and wind. However, they might not offer much protection from the cold, so use them as a temporary solution while looking for a more secure location.

Making Urban Shelters More Comfortable and Safe

Once you find a shelter, improving its comfort and safety can help you stay secure:

1. **Using Found Materials:**
   - **Cardboard and Plastic Sheeting:** Gather these materials to create insulation from the cold or rain. Cardboard can help block wind and plastic sheeting can keep you dry.

2. **Staying Hidden but Accessible:**
   - **Visibility:** Choose a spot that's hidden enough to keep you safe but still visible to potential rescuers. Avoid areas that are too isolated or dangerous.

3. **Keeping a Low Profile:**
   - **Avoid Danger:** Stay away from areas that are risky or where there's heavy traffic. Keeping a low profile helps you stay safe and avoid drawing unnecessary attention.

4. **Maintaining Cleanliness:**
   - **Safety:** Keep your shelter area as clean as possible to avoid attracting pests or becoming ill. Proper cleanliness is especially important in urban environments where sanitation might be a concern.

5. **Seeking Help:**
   - **Emergency Contacts:** If you can, use a phone or any other means to contact emergency services or people who can help. Make sure you know how to use these tools in an emergency.

By understanding these concepts and being prepared, you can navigate urban environments safely and find effective shelter when you need it most.

Signaling for Help While in Urban Shelters

When you're in an urban shelter, knowing how to signal for help is essential. Whether you're waiting for rescue or trying to get the attention of passersby, these skills can make a big difference. Here's how you can attract attention safely and effectively.

1. **Using Whistles or Loud Noises**

Whistles:

- **Why Use a Whistle:** A whistle can carry sound much further than your voice and can be heard over distances and background noise.
- **How to Use It:** Blow the whistle in short bursts—three short blasts is the international signal for distress. Hold the whistle firmly and make sure it's not blocked.

2. **Loud Noises:**

- **Shouting:** If you don't have a whistle, shouting can help. Make sure to shout in short, loud bursts to avoid getting too tired.
- **Clapping or Bang Objects:** Use objects like a stick or metal can to create loud sounds. Bang them together rhythmically or in irregular patterns to draw attention.

3. **Creating Visible Signals**

Bright Clothing:

- **Use Bright Colors:** Wear or display bright-colored clothing, like a red or orange jacket, which can stand out against the urban background.
- **Layer Visibility:** Hang these items where they are easily seen, such as from a window or high point.

Reflective Materials:

- **Use Reflective Items:** If you have reflective materials like emergency blankets or strips, place them where they catch light. Reflective materials shine brightly when light hits them, especially from headlights or streetlights.
- **Create Patterns:** Arrange reflective items in patterns or shapes that can be easily seen from a distance.

Knowing Emergency Contact Numbers and Landmarks

Emergency Contact Numbers

- **Have Important Numbers Ready:** Know the local emergency services number (e.g., 911 in the United States). Memorize or keep a list of emergency contacts with you.
- **Write It Down:** Keep a written copy of emergency numbers in a safe place, like a waterproof bag, or memorize them if you can.

Landmarks

- **Identify Nearby Landmarks:** If you're in a known location, identify nearby landmarks that could help rescuers locate you. This could include major buildings, parks, or well-known streets.

- **Describe Your Location:** If you need to call for help, be ready to describe where you are. Use landmarks or features of the area to help others find you quickly.

> ### Extra Tips for Signaling for Help
>
> - **Stay Calm:** Keeping calm helps you think clearly and use your signaling tools effectively.
>
> - **Repeat Signals:** If you don't get a response right away, repeat your signals at regular intervals.
>
> - **Visibility and Audibility:** Make sure your signals are both visible and audible from as far away as possible.

By learning these signaling techniques, you'll be better prepared to get noticed and stay safe in an urban emergency. Remember, being prepared and knowing how to use these tools can make a big difference in getting the help you need. Stay alert, and always be ready to signal for help if you find yourself in a tough spot!

Quiz:
Chapter 6 - Shelters

Short Answer Questions

1. What is a lean-to shelter and why is it called that?

2. List three materials needed to build a lean-to shelter.

3. Why is it important to check for gaps in your shelter?

4. What should you do if you find cracks or weak spots in a snow shelter?

5. Describe two types of snow shelters and one unique feature of each.

Multiple Choice Questions

1. What is the primary purpose of a lean-to shelter?

a) To keep you warm and dry
b) To provide a place to cook food
c) To store equipment
d) To find food

2. Which material is NOT typically used to build a lean-to shelter?

a) Long, sturdy branches
b) Small rocks
c) Leaves and pine needles
d) Natural cordage

3. When building a debris hut, what is the purpose of the ridgepole?

a) To form the base of the hut
b) To act as a roof support
c) To create insulation
d) To block out sunlight

4. Which type of snow shelter is built by piling and compacting snow?

a) Igloo
b) Quinzee
c) Lean-to
d) Debris Hut

5. What is a key feature of urban shelters when you are in a city?

a) They must be highly visible
b) They should be located in a public park
c) They need to be clean and comfortable
d) They should be hidden and safe

True or False Questions

1. A lean-to shelter is built by leaning branches against a support like a tree or rock. (True/False)
2. For a debris hut, you should create a small entrance to keep the heat inside. (True/False)
3. Snow shelters like igloos are built using snow blocks that are stacked in a dome shape. (True/False)
4. It is not necessary to create ventilation holes in a quinzee. (True/False)
5. In an urban shelter, using bright clothing can help you be more visible to rescuers. (True/False)

Chapter 7
Survival Gear

When you're out exploring the wilderness or even just navigating through a city, having the right survival gear can make all the difference. Here's a guide to the essential items you should have in different environments and why they're so important. is a must-have to keep you both comfortable and safe.

Essential Survival Gear for Different Environments

Basic Wilderness Survival Kit:

- **Knife:** A sturdy, sharp knife is one of the most versatile tools you can carry. You can use it for cutting, carving, preparing food, and even making other tools.
- **Fire Starter:** Matches, a lighter, or a flint and steel are crucial for starting a fire. A fire provides warmth, helps you cook food, and can signal for help.
- **Whistle:** A whistle is a simple but effective way to signal for help. Its sound travels farther than your voice, making it easier for rescuers to find you.
- **First Aid Kit:** A small first aid kit with bandages, antiseptic wipes, and other basic medical supplies helps you treat minor injuries until you can get more help.
- **Water Bottle or Purification Tablets:** Staying hydrated is vital. If you can't carry enough water, purification tablets can make water from natural sources safe to drink.
- **Map and Compass:** These tools help you navigate and find your way back to safety if you get lost.

Urban Survival Kit:

- **Maps:** In an urban environment, a map of the area is essential for finding your way, especially if you're in an unfamiliar city.
- **Emergency Contacts:** Keep a list of emergency contacts, including family, friends, and local authorities, so you can quickly reach out for help.
- **Small Flashlight:** A flashlight is important for seeing in the dark and signaling for help. Choose a small, lightweight one that fits easily in your pocket or bag.
- **Multi-tool:** Similar to a knife but more versatile, a multi-tool includes various functions like scissors, pliers, and screwdrivers, which can be useful in many situations.
- **Whistle:** Just like in the wilderness, a whistle is crucial for signaling in an urban environment, especially if you're in a noisy area.

Why Each Item is Important

Fire Starter:

- **Purpose:** A fire starter is crucial for creating warmth, cooking food, and signaling for help. In cold environments, it can prevent hypothermia, and in any situation, it can be used to cook or purify water.
- **Importance:** Knowing how to start a fire can make your survival much easier and more comfortable.

Whistle:

- **Purpose:** A whistle is a reliable tool for attracting attention if you're lost or in danger. Its loud, high-pitched sound can be heard from a distance, alerting rescuers to your location.
- **Importance:** It's much easier and less tiring to blow a whistle than to yell for help, especially over long periods.

First Aid Kit:

- **Purpose:** A first aid kit helps you treat cuts, scrapes, burns, and other injuries. Having basic medical supplies on hand allows you to take care of minor issues before they become major problems.
- **Importance:** In a survival situation, staying healthy is crucial. A first aid kit helps you address injuries quickly and effectively.

Map and Compass:

- **Purpose:** These navigation tools help you find your way in both wilderness and urban environments. They are essential for ensuring you don't get lost and can find your way back to safety.
- **Importance:** Even if you have a great sense of direction, a map and compass are reliable tools to have, especially in unfamiliar areas.

Customizing Your Survival Kit

- Every environment is different, and so are your needs. Here's how to customize your survival kit based on where you are and what you might face:

1. **Different Climates:**
   - **Cold Weather Gear:** If you're in a cold environment, pack extra layers of clothing, a hat, gloves, and even a space blanket to stay warm.
   - **Sun Protection:** In hot or sunny climates, include sunscreen, sunglasses, and a hat to protect yourself from sunburn and heat exhaustion.

2. **Personal Items:**
   - **Medications:** If you have any special medical needs, make sure to include necessary medications in your kit.
   - **Comfort Items:** Sometimes a small comfort item, like a family photo or a favorite snack, can make a big difference in keeping your spirits up in a tough situation.

By understanding the purpose of each item and tailoring your survival kit to your specific needs and environment, you'll be better prepared for any situation. Remember, the most important tool you have is your mind, so always think ahead and stay calm.

How to Pack and Maintain Your Survival Kit

Packing and maintaining your survival kit is just as important as knowing how to use it. A well-prepared and organized kit can make a big difference when you need it most. Here's how you can make sure your survival kit is always ready to go.

Regularly Checking and Replacing Expired Items

Your survival kit is full of important items, but some of them, like food, water, and medical supplies, can expire or go bad over time.

Check Expiration Dates:

- **Food and Water:** If you have food bars, snacks, or water bottles in your kit, make sure to check their expiration dates regularly. Replace any items that are close to expiring so that they're always safe to eat or drink.
- **First Aid Supplies:** Some first aid items, like ointments, medications, or bandages, can also expire. Check these regularly and replace them when needed to ensure they work properly when you need them.

Inspect for Damage:

- **Tools and Gear:** Take a look at your tools, like your knife, flashlight, and fire starter, to make sure they're not damaged. If you find any issues, replace them or fix them so they're ready when you need them.
- **Containers and Bags:** Check the bag or container where you keep your survival kit. Make sure it's not torn or damaged and that it's still waterproof if needed.

Ensuring Items are Easily Accessible and Organized

When you're in a hurry, you don't want to waste time searching through your kit to find what you need. Keeping your kit organized and easy to access is key.

1. **Pack Smart:**

   - **Layering:** Place the items you're most likely to need first, like a flashlight, whistle, or first aid supplies, on top or in easily accessible pockets.
   - **Grouping:** Group similar items together, like all first aid supplies in one pouch and all fire-starting tools in another. This way, you can quickly find what you need.

2. **Use Labels or Clear Bags:**

   - **Labels:** If your kit has multiple pockets or compartments, consider labeling them so you know where everything is. For example, you could label one pocket "First Aid" and another "Tools."
   - **Clear Bags:** Using clear, resealable bags to store smaller items like matches, bandages, or snacks can help you see what's inside without having to dig through everything.

3. **Practice Packing and Unpacking:**

   - **Practice Runs:** It's a good idea to practice packing and unpacking your kit so you know exactly where everything is. This will also help you get faster at finding items in an emergency.

4. **Keep Your Kit in a Safe, Accessible Place:**

   - **Home and On-the-Go:** Whether your kit is at home or you're carrying it with you, make sure it's stored in a place where you can grab it quickly if needed. For example, keep it by the door or in a designated spot in your backpack.

Staying Ready

- Maintaining your survival kit isn't something you do just once—it's an ongoing process. Make it a habit to check your kit regularly, at least every few months, to ensure everything is in good shape and ready to use.

- By taking care of your survival kit, you're making sure that you'll be prepared for whatever comes your way. Remember, being ready is about more than just having the right gear—it's also about keeping that gear in top condition and knowing where to find it when you need it.

Ultimate Survival & Wilderness Skills for Kids

Quiz:
Chapter 7 – Survival Gear

Multiple Choice Questions

1. How does a first aid kit help in a survival situation?

a) It helps you signal for help
b) It provides tools to catch food
c) It helps you treat minor injuries before they become major problems
d) It helps start a fire quickly

2. What makes a whistle more effective than yelling for help?

a) It uses less energy and can be heard from farther away
b) It scares off animals
c) It makes a deeper, more resonant sound
d) It lasts longer

3. Why is a fire starter important in cold environments?

a) It helps you cook better meals
b) It can help prevent hypothermia
c) It helps dry wet clothes
d) It scares away animals

4. Why is it important to carry a map and compass even if you have a good sense of direction?

a) They help you make friends in the wilderness
b) They provide more accurate information in unfamiliar areas
c) They can be used to start a fire
d) They are easier to use than modern GPS systems

5. Why is it important to regularly check the expiration dates of food and water in your survival kit?

a) To reduce weight in the kit
b) To ensure they are safe to eat or drink
c) To improve their taste
d) To comply with legal regulations

True or False Questions

1. First aid supplies, such as ointments and medications, can expire and should be replaced when necessary. (True/False)

2. Inspecting your survival tools, like a knife or flashlight, is unnecessary if they are stored properly. (True/False)

3. A map and compass are useful only in wilderness environments. (True/False)

4. Practicing how to pack and unpack your kit can help you become faster at finding items during an emergency. (True/False)

Chapter 8
Navigation and Signaling Skills

Learning to use a compass is a valuable skill that can help you navigate through the wilderness or an unfamiliar area. Here's how a compass works, how to use it, and how it can guide you to safety.

A compass is a simple tool that helps you find your way by pointing to the Earth's magnetic north. Let's look at the key parts of a compass:

Understanding the Basic Parts of a Compass

- **The Needle and Its Magnetic Properties:** The needle is a thin, metal arrow that floats on a pivot inside the compass. One end of the needle is usually colored (often red) and always points to magnetic north. This is because the needle is magnetized and aligns with the Earth's magnetic field.

- **The Rotating Bezel and Degree Markings:** The bezel is a circular ring around the edge of the compass that you can turn. It has degree markings from 0° to 360° that help you determine the direction you want to go. The north marking on the bezel is usually highlighted or has a special symbol.

- **The Baseplate and Direction of Travel Arrow:** The baseplate is the flat, clear part of the compass that you hold in your hand. On the baseplate, there is a direction of travel arrow, which shows the way you should go when you're following a bearing (a specific direction).

How to Hold and Read a Compass Properly

Now that you know the parts of a compass, let's learn how to hold and read it correctly:

1. **Holding the Compass Flat and Level in Your Hand:**
   - Hold the compass flat and level in the palm of your hand, so the needle can spin freely. If the compass tilts, the needle might get stuck and give you an inaccurate reading.

2. **Aligning the Needle with the North Marking on the Bezel:**
   - Turn the compass and your body until the red end of the needle lines up with the north marking on the bezel. This tells you that the compass is oriented correctly, with the top of the compass pointing north.

3. **Understanding the Degree Readings for Different Directions:**
   - Look at the degree markings on the bezel. North is usually 0° or 360°, east is 90°, south is 180°, and west is 270°. These readings help you know which direction you're facing or need to travel.

Step-by-Step Instructions for Taking a Bearing

Taking a bearing means finding the exact direction you want to travel using your compass. Here's how to do it:

1. **Choosing a Landmark and Pointing the Compass at It:**
   - Pick a visible landmark in the direction you want to go, like a tree, rock, or mountain. Hold the compass in front of you and point the direction of travel arrow at the landmark.

2. **Rotating the Bezel Until the Needle Aligns with the North Marking:**
   - Without moving the compass, turn the bezel until the red end of the needle lines up with the north marking. The direction of travel arrow should still point at your landmark.

3. **Reading the Degree Marking at the Direction of Travel Arrow:**
   - Look at the number on the bezel where the direction of travel arrow points. This is your bearing, or the degree direction you should follow.

4. **Following the Bearing While Keeping the Needle Aligned:**
    - Start walking toward your landmark while keeping an eye on the compass.
    - Make sure the needle stays aligned with the north marking on the bezel.
    - This ensures you're staying on course.

By mastering these compass skills, you'll be able to find your way in the wilderness, even without a map or GPS.

Practical Tips for Using a Compass in the Field

When you're out exploring or in a survival situation, knowing how to use your compass effectively is key to staying on the right path.

Checking the Compass Regularly to Stay on Course

It's important to check your compass often while walking to make sure you're still heading in the right direction. Terrain can sometimes make it hard to go in a straight line, so by checking your compass frequently, you can avoid accidentally veering off course.

Using a Map in Conjunction with the Compass for Better Accuracy

A compass is a powerful tool on its own, but when you use it with a map, you can navigate even more accurately. By lining up your map with the compass, you can see exactly where you are and where you need to go. This helps you plan the best route and avoid obstacles like rivers or steep terrain.

Avoiding Metal Objects and Electronic Devices That Can Interfere with the Compass

Metal objects, such as knives or metal poles, and electronic devices like smartphones can mess up your compass reading by pulling the needle away from true north. When you use your compass, hold it away from anything metal or electronic to ensure an accurate reading.

Navigating by the Sun

In addition to using a compass, you can also navigate by the sun. This method is especially helpful if you don't have a compass or need to confirm the direction your compass is pointing.

The Sun's Movement from East to West

- The sun rises in the east and sets in the west. This means that in the morning, the sun will be in the eastern part of the sky, and in the evening, it will be in the western part. By knowing this, you can use the sun to find your direction.

Understanding the Position of the Sun at Different Times of the Day

- Around midday, the sun is generally to the south in the northern hemisphere and to the north in the southern hemisphere. By paying attention to where the sun is in the sky, you can estimate your direction at any time of the day.

Using the Sun's Position to Find Cardinal Directions

- If you know where the sun is in the sky, you can figure out the four main directions: north, south, east, and west. For example, if it's morning and the sun is in front of you, you're likely facing east.

How to Use the Shadow Stick Navigation Method

The shadow stick method is a simple way to use the sun to find direction.

1. **Finding a Straight Stick and Placing It Vertically in the Ground**

- Look for a straight stick, about 1 to 2 feet long, and push it upright into the ground where it casts a clear shadow.

2. **Marking the Tip of the Shadow with a Small Rock or Stick**

- Notice where the tip of the stick's shadow falls on the ground. Place a small rock, stick, or other marker at that spot. This first mark shows where the shadow is in the morning.

3. **Waiting 15-30 Minutes and Marking the New Tip of the Shadow**

- After waiting for 15 to 30 minutes, you'll see that the shadow has moved. Mark the new position of the shadow's tip.

4. **Drawing a Line Between the Two Marks to Create an East-West Line**

- Draw a line connecting the two marks. This line runs roughly east to west, with the first mark showing the western end and the second mark showing the eastern end.

Using an Analog Watch for Solar Navigation

Did you know that you can use an analog watch (one with hour and minute hands) to help you find your way using the sun? This method is a handy skill to have if you don't have a compass with you. Here's how you can use a watch to figure out the north-south direction.

1. **Holding the Watch Horizontally with the Hour Hand Pointing at the Sun**

- First, hold your analog watch flat and level in your hand so that the face of the watch is parallel to the ground.

- Then, turn the watch or your wrist until the hour hand (the short hand) is pointing directly at the sun. Make sure the watch is in the correct time zone and showing the correct time.

2. **Bisecting the Angle Between the Hour Hand and the 12 o'clock Mark to Find the North-South Line**

- Imagine an invisible line that runs between the hour hand (pointing at the sun) and the 12 o'clock mark on your watch.

- Now, find the middle point of this angle. This middle point, or "bisector," gives you the north-south line.

- In the northern hemisphere, the midpoint between the hour hand and the 12 o'clock mark points south, and the opposite direction points north.

3. **Adjusting the Method for Different Hemispheres (Northern vs. Southern)**

- If you're in the southern hemisphere, the method is slightly different.

Instead of pointing the hour hand at the sun, point the 12 o'clock mark at the sun. The midpoint between the hour hand and the 12 o'clock mark will then give you the north-south line. In this case, the midpoint direction closest to the sun is north, and the opposite direction is south.

> ### Practical Tips for Solar Navigation in Different Environments
>
> Solar navigation is a great skill, but it's important to use it wisely depending on where you are and the time of year. Here are some tips to help you navigate effectively using the sun and a watch.
>
> **Using Natural Landmarks to Confirm Direction**
>
> When navigating using the sun, always try to confirm your direction by checking natural landmarks around you, like mountains, rivers, or distinct trees. This will help you double-check your findings and stay on course.
>
> **Considering the Time of Year and the Sun's Angle in the Sky**
>
> Remember that the sun's position in the sky changes with the seasons. In summer, the sun is higher in the sky, while in winter, it's lower. Be mindful of these changes when using solar navigation, as they can slightly affect your direction finding.
>
> **Combining Solar Navigation with Other Techniques for Better Accuracy**
>
> While using the sun and a watch is helpful, it's always a good idea to combine this method with other navigation techniques, like using a compass or observing the stars at night, for the most accurate results.

Night Navigation – Using the Stars

Navigating at night can seem tricky, but with a little knowledge of the stars, you can find your way even in the dark! The stars have been used for navigation for thousands of years because they follow predictable patterns in the sky. In this section of Navigating and Signaling Skills, you'll learn how to use the stars to guide you when the sun goes down.

Celestial Navigation: Finding Your Way with Starst

Celestial navigation is all about using the stars to figure out where you are and where you need to go. Certain stars and constellations (groups of stars that form patterns) are particularly helpful because they stay in fixed positions or move in predictable ways throughout the night. These star patterns are reliable guides that can help you determine direction, especially if you're in a place without other landmarks.

Finding the North Star (Polaris)

One of the most important stars to know is Polaris, also known as the North Star. Polaris is special because it stays almost directly above the North Pole, which means it always points to true north. Here's how you can find it:

1. **Identify the Big Dipper Constellation:**

   ◦ Look for the Big Dipper, a bright group of seven stars that form a shape like a large spoon or dipper. The Big Dipper is part of a larger constellation called Ursa Major, the Great Bear.

2. **Use the "Pointer" Stars to Find Polaris:**

   ◦ Find the two stars at the end of the Big Dipper's bowl. These are called the "pointer" stars because they point the way to Polaris.

   ◦ Imagine a straight line running through these two stars and follow that line upward. Polaris is the first bright star you'll see along that line.

3. **Understand That Polaris Indicates True North:**
   - Once you've found Polaris, you know that you're facing true north. From there, south will be directly behind you, east to your right, and west to your left.

Using Other Constellations for Navigation

While Polaris is great for finding north, other constellations can also help you navigate.

The Southern Cross (Southern Hemisphere):
   - If you're in the southern hemisphere, you won't be able to see Polaris, but you can use the Southern Cross, a small but bright constellation.
   - To find south, draw an imaginary line from the top of the cross down through the bottom, and extend it to the horizon. This line points roughly to the south.

Orion's Belt:
   - Orion is a well-known constellation visible from both the northern and southern hemispheres. It's easy to spot because of the three bright stars that form Orion's Belt.
   - If you draw an imaginary line through Orion's Belt, it points in the direction of the east-west line. The belt rises in the east and sets in the west.

The Milky Way:
   - The Milky Way is a dense band of stars that stretches across the sky. It can help you navigate by providing a clear and recognizable landmark in the night sky.
   - Depending on the time of year and your location, the Milky Way can help you determine the general direction of north-south or east-west.

Practical Tips for Effective Night Navigation

To navigate successfully at night using the stars, here are some important tips to keep in mind:

- **Allow Your Eyes to Adjust to the Darkness:** It takes about 20-30 minutes for your eyes to fully adjust to the dark, so be patient and avoid looking at bright lights during this time.

- **Use a Red Light Flashlight:** If you need to use a flashlight, choose one with a red light. Red light doesn't affect your night vision as much as white light, so you'll still be able to see the stars clearly.

- **Practice Star Navigation on Clear Nights:** The best way to get good at star navigation is to practice! On clear nights, go outside with a star chart or a guide to help you learn the constellations and how they move.

By learning how to navigate using the stars, you'll gain a skill that not only helps you find your way but also connects you with the night sky in a whole new way. Whether you're camping, hiking, or just out for an adventure, knowing how to use the stars can be a fun and practical tool in your survival skills toolkit.

Creating and Following Natural Landmarks

When you're out exploring, whether in the wilderness or in an unfamiliar part of town, natural landmarks can be your best friends. They help you find your way and make sure you don't get lost. In this chapter, we'll learn how to use the natural features around you to navigate, how to create your own landmarks, and how to follow them to stay on track.

The Importance of Natural Landmarks in Navigation

Natural landmarks are features in the environment that stand out and are easy to recognize. They are reliable because they don't move or change quickly, making them excellent reference points when you're trying to find your way. Here's why they're so important:

Using Prominent Features:

- Look for big, noticeable things in your surroundings, like mountains, rivers, or large trees. These are natural landmarks that you can use to guide yourself.
- For example, if you're hiking and there's a big mountain to the east, you can use it to make sure you're going in the right direction. If you keep that mountain on your left, you'll know you're heading south.

Understanding Consistency:

- Natural landmarks don't change much over time. A large rock formation, a bend in a river, or a distinct tree will likely be there for years.
- This consistency means that once you've identified a landmark, you can rely on it to help you navigate back the way you came or move forward on your path.

Creating Your Own Landmarks

Sometimes, the natural landmarks around you might not be enough, especially if you're in a dense forest or an area without many distinguishing features. That's when creating your own landmarks can be super helpful. Here's how to do it:

1. **Stacking Rocks (Cairns):**
   - A cairn is a small pile of rocks stacked on top of each other. You can create cairns at regular intervals along your path to mark your trail.
   - Be sure to use rocks that stand out and stack them high enough to be easily seen.

2. **Blazing Trees:**
   - Blazing a tree means marking it in a way that others (and you) can recognize. You can use a knife to carve a small mark or strip a bit of bark from the tree.
   - Always be careful not to harm the tree too much; just make a mark that's easy to spot as you retrace your steps.

3. **Using Ribbons or Cloth:**
   - Tie a ribbon or a strip of cloth to branches along your path. Make sure the material is brightly colored so it's easy to see.

- This method is especially useful if you're moving through an area with thick vegetation where other landmarks might be hard to find.

Following Natural Landmarks

Now that you know how to identify and create landmarks, let's talk about how to use them to navigate:

1. **Identifying and Remembering Key Landmarks:**
   - As you travel, take note of the most prominent and unique features you see. It could be a tree with an unusual shape, a big boulder, or a bend in the river.
   - Try to remember these landmarks by associating them with something familiar, like, "That tree looks like a giant Y" or "This rock is shaped like a turtle."

2. **Noting Unique Features:**
   - Pay attention to details like color, shape, and size. If a tree is particularly tall or has bright-colored leaves, it can be a great landmark.
   - By focusing on these unique characteristics, you'll have an easier time remembering and finding your way back if needed.

3. **Creating Mental Maps:**
   - As you move, start creating a mental map by connecting the landmarks in a sequence. For example, "First, I pass the big oak tree, then I cross the stream, and finally, I reach the large rock."
   - This mental map helps you navigate more confidently because you'll have a clear path in your mind.

Practical Examples of Using Landmarks in Different Environments

Natural landmarks are everywhere, but how you use them depends on where you are. Let's look at some examples:

In Wilderness Areas:
- **Rivers and Rock Formations:** When hiking or camping, rivers are excellent landmarks. You can follow a river downstream to find civilization or use unique rock formations to navigate through a forest.
- **Vegetation Patterns:** Notice how the vegetation changes as you move. A dense patch of ferns or a grove of pine trees can help mark your location.

In Urban Settings:
- **Street Signs and Building Features:** In a city or town, street signs, large buildings, or even specific types of architecture can act as landmarks. For example, you might remember, "Turn left at the building with the green roof" or "Head straight until you see the bakery."
- **Parks and Statues:** Parks with large statues, fountains, or playgrounds can also be useful landmarks to help you find your way around.

In Different Climates:
- **Deserts:** In a desert, large dunes, distinct rock formations, or an oasis can be your guiding landmarks. The shadows cast by these features can also help you navigate.

- **Snowy Environments:** In snowy areas, landmarks might include large snowdrifts, tree lines, or even the way the snow has drifted around specific objects.

The P.A.U.L. Navigation Method: A Simple Way to Find Your Way

When you're exploring or trying to find your way, it's super helpful to have a simple and easy-to-remember method. One such method is the P.A.U.L. Navigation Method. This method stands for Position, Aim, Understand, and Look. It's a great tool for kids aged 7 to 14 to use when navigating through different environments, whether you're in the wilderness or just trying to find your way around a new place. Let's break down each part of the P.A.U.L. method and learn how to use it effectively.

P: Position

The first step in the P.A.U.L. method is figuring out where you are. This is called Position.

1. **Identify Your Current Location:**
   - Look around you and identify any landmarks or features that you recognize. Are there any tall trees, big rocks, or distinctive buildings nearby?
   - If you have a map or a compass, use them to pinpoint your location.

2. **Use Available Tools:**
   - If you have a map, locate your position on it. If you're using a compass, make sure you know which direction you're facing.
   - Remember, it's important to stay calm and take a good look around to get a clear idea of your surroundings.

A: Aim

The next step is Aim. This means deciding where you want to go.

1. **Determine Your Destination:**
   - Think about where you want to end up. Is there a specific landmark you're trying to reach, like a river, a mountain, or a building?
   - Set a clear goal for your navigation. For example, you might aim to find a picnic spot, a specific trail, or even get back home.

2. **Plan Your Route:**
   - Once you know where you want to go, plan the best route to get there.
   - Look for natural pathways or landmarks that will guide you.
   - Decide if you need to move straight towards your goal or if there are obstacles you need to navigate around.

U: Understand

The Understand step is all about figuring out how to get from your current position to your destination.

1. **Evaluate Your Route:**
    - Look at your planned route and think about what you'll encounter along the way. Are there any hills, rivers, or dense bushes?
    - Consider what kind of terrain you'll be walking on and how that might affect your journey.

2. **Use Navigation Tools:**
    - If you have a compass, use it to check the direction you need to go. If you're following a map, trace your route and note any important features.
    - Make sure you understand how to use any tools you have, like a map or compass, to keep you on the right path.

L: Look

The final step is Look. This means staying observant and making adjustments as needed.

1. **Observe Your Surroundings:**
    - As you move, keep an eye out for landmarks that match those on your map or that you identified earlier.
    - Regularly check your route and make sure you're still on track. Look for any changes in the terrain or new obstacles.

2. **Adjust as Necessary:**
    - If you find that your route isn't working out as planned, don't panic. Use the landmarks and features around you to adjust your path.
    - Be flexible and ready to change your route if needed. Sometimes things don't go as planned, and that's okay!

Practical Tips for Using the P.A.U.L. Method

Practice Makes Perfect:

The more you practice using the P.A.U.L. method, the better you'll get at navigating. Try using it on hikes, nature walks, or even in your own backyard.

Stay Safe:

Always make sure you're in a safe environment when practicing navigation. If you're exploring new areas, let someone know where you're going and take safety precautions.

Combine with Other Skills:

The P.A.U.L. method works great on its own, but you can also combine it with other navigation skills like using a compass or identifying natural landmarks.

Have Fun:

Navigating can be a fun adventure! Enjoy discovering new places and learning how to find your way using the P.A.U.L. method.

Emergency Signaling: Using Mirrors and Reflective

When you find yourself in an emergency situation, being able to signal for help is crucial. One effective method for signaling is using mirrors or reflective surfaces. Mirrors can reflect sunlight over long distances, making them a powerful tool for attracting attention and getting rescued.

Understanding Mirror Signaling

How Mirrors Reflect Light:

Reflection Principle:

Mirrors work by bouncing light off their surface. When sunlight hits a mirror, it reflects in the direction you're aiming. This reflection can travel far distances and be seen by people who are looking in the right direction.

Intensity of Sunlight:

Bright sunlight provides the best conditions for mirror signaling. The stronger the sunlight, the more visible your signal will be.

Materials Needed for Mirror Signaling

1. **Signal Mirrors:**

    - **Signal Mirrors with Sighting Holes:** These mirrors are designed specifically for signaling and often come with a small hole in the center to help you aim.

2. **Improvised Mirrors:**

    - **Compact Mirrors:** These are often found in personal grooming kits and can be used effectively in emergencies.

- **Polished Metal Surfaces:** Items like metal cookware or metal tins can be used if they have a shiny surface.

- **CDs/DVDs:** The reflective surface of a CD or DVD can also be used to signal for help.

Step-by-Step Instructions for Using a Signal Mirror

1. **Holding the Mirror Correctly:**

    - **Position:** Hold the mirror flat and level in your hand. Ensure it catches the sunlight directly. If you're using an improvised mirror, make sure it's clean and shiny.

2. **Aiming the Reflection:**

    - **Using the Sighting Hole:** If your mirror has a sighting hole, look through it and aim the reflection at your target. This helps you direct the light more accurately.

    - **Without a Sighting Hole:** If your mirror doesn't have a sighting hole, use the reflection's movement to guide the light. Move the mirror slowly and adjust until you see the reflection hitting your target.

3. **Creating Flashes:**

    - **Flashing Technique:** To attract attention, you'll need to create a pattern of flashes. Move the mirror back and forth to make the reflection blink on and off. This helps in catching the attention of searchers who might be looking from a distance.

Tips for Effective Mirror Signaling

Choose a Clear, Sunny Day:

Best Conditions: Mirrors work best on sunny days when sunlight is strong. Cloudy or rainy weather can make it harder to see the reflection.

Use a Series of Flashes:

Recognizable Patterns: To make your signal stand out, use a pattern of short and long flashes. For example, three short flashes followed by a long one can signal distress and make your signal more noticeable.

Aim at High Points:

Best Targets: Try to aim your mirror signal at high points, such as mountaintops or aircraft. These are more likely to be seen by rescuers who are searching from the air or from a distance.

Keep Your Mirror Accessible:

Easy Access: If you're in an emergency situation, keep your mirror within easy reach. You may need to use it quickly if you spot a searcher or hear rescuers approaching.

Practice and Familiarity

Practice with Your Mirror:

Familiarization: Spend some time practicing with your mirror in a safe environment. Get comfortable with how to hold it and aim the reflection.

Know Your Environment:

Adaptation: Understand the surroundings where you might need to use your mirror. Practice aiming at different types of targets, such as buildings or trees, to improve your signaling skills.

By using mirrors and reflective surfaces effectively, you can increase your chances of being seen and getting the help you need in an emergency. Remember to stay calm, use your mirror wisely, and practice these techniques so you'll be ready if you ever find yourself in a tough situation.

Whistle Signals – What They Mean

In an emergency, one of the most effective tools for getting noticed is a whistle. Whistles are powerful because they can be heard over long distances and don't require a lot of physical effort to use. Let's dive into why whistles are so important, the standard signals you should know, and how to use them effectively.

The Importance of Whistle Signals in Emergencies

Advantages of Using a Whistle:

- **Loud and Piercing:** A whistle can make a loud, piercing sound that travels far and cuts through other noises. This makes it easier for rescuers to hear you even if they're far away.

- **Low Effort:** Using a whistle requires less physical effort compared to shouting or waving. This can be crucial when you're tired or in a difficult situation.

- **Reliable:** A whistle won't wear out or lose its effectiveness like your voice might over time. It's a dependable tool for attracting attention.

Standard Whistle Signal Codes

Knowing the right whistle signals can help you communicate clearly in an emergency. Here are the basic codes to remember:

1. **Three Short Blasts:**
    - **Meaning:** Distress or Emergency
    - **When to Use:** If you're in immediate danger and need urgent help. This is a universal distress signal that tells others you need assistance right away.

2. **Two Short Blasts:**
    - **Meaning:** Attention or Gathering
    - **When to Use:** To alert others to your presence or to call a group together. This signal is useful for non-emergency communication.

3. **One Long Blast:**
   - **Meaning:** Location Confirmation
   - **When to Use:** To let others know where you are or to confirm that you've been spotted. This helps rescuers identify your position.

Materials Needed for Effective Whistle Signaling

1. **Types of Whistles:**
   - **Pealess Whistles:** These are loud and reliable because they don't have a moving ball inside. They're great for clear, consistent sounds.
   - **Whistles with Built-In Features:** Some whistles come with extra tools like compasses or small lights, which can be helpful in emergencies.
   - Improvised Whistles: If you don't have a whistle, you can make a simple one from bamboo or hollowed wood. These won't be as effective but can be useful in a pinch.

2. **Characteristics of Good Whistles:**
   - **Loudness:** Make sure the whistle is loud enough to be heard from a distance.
   - **Durability:** Choose a whistle that can withstand tough conditions, such as water and rough handling.
   - **Ease of Use:** It should be easy to blow and handle, especially in stressful situations.

Practical Tips for Using Whistles Effectively

Practice Signal Codes Regularly:

Get Comfortable: Practice blowing your whistle and using the different signals so you'll remember them easily in an emergency.

In Different Conditions: Try practicing in various environments to understand how well your whistle carries sound.

Keep the Whistle Accessible:

Location: Always keep your whistle within easy reach. Attach it to a lanyard or put it in a pocket so you can grab it quickly if needed.

Visibility: Make sure it's visible and not buried under other gear.

Use with Other Signals:

Combine Signals: Use your whistle along with other signaling methods, like mirrors or smoke signals, to increase your chances of being seen or heard.

Make Noise: If you see rescuers or hear someone nearby, use your whistle to make noise and draw their attention.

Creating Smoke Signals

Smoke signals are an ancient and effective way to communicate over long distances. Used by various cultures throughout history, they are a great survival skill to know so you can signal for help during an emergency.

The Significance of Smoke Signals

Historical and Practical Use:

- **Visibility Over Distances:** Smoke signals are visible from afar, making them useful for sending messages when you can't use radios or phones. They can be seen from miles away if the conditions are right.
- **Historical Examples:** Indigenous peoples, such as Native American tribes, used smoke signals to send messages and warnings across vast distances. Military units also employed them to coordinate and communicate during various conflicts.

Materials Needed for Creating Smoke Signals

1. **Dry Wood and Kindling:**
   - **Purpose:** These materials are used to start and maintain the base fire.
   - **Types:** Gather dry twigs, branches, and small logs for a strong, steady fire.
2. **Green Branches, Leaves, or Grass:**
   - **Purpose:** Adding green materials produces thick, white smoke, which is more visible.
   - **Types:** Collect leaves, green branches, and grasses. The greener and wetter they are, the more smoke they'll produce.
3. **A Large, Open Area:**
   - **Purpose:** Ensures that smoke can disperse without obstruction and increases the chances of it being seen.
   - **Types:** Choose an area away from trees, buildings, or other obstacles that might block the smoke.

Step-by-Step Instructions for Building a Smoke Signal Fire

1. **Create a Small, Controlled Base Fire:**
   - **Gather Materials:** Collect dry wood and kindling. Arrange the kindling in a small pile and place the dry wood around it.
   - **Start the Fire:** Light the kindling with a fire starter or matches. Gradually add more wood to build up the fire.
2. **Add Green Materials for Smoke:**
   - **Prepare Green Materials:** Break or tear the green branches, leaves, or grass into smaller pieces.
   - **Add to Fire:** Once the base fire is burning well, carefully place the green materials on top. They will start to smolder and produce thick, white smoke.

3. **Use a Blanket or Tarp to Control Smoke:**
   - **Position the Cover:** Hold a blanket or tarp above the fire to trap and then release the smoke in puffs.
   - **Create Puffs:** Lift and lower the blanket or tarp to create a series of smoke puffs. Each puff of smoke can be seen from a distance and helps convey your message.

Tips for Effective Smoke Signaling

Choose the Right Conditions:

Clear, Calm Day: Smoke signals are most visible on clear, calm days.

Avoid windy days as wind can blow the smoke away and reduce visibility.

Create a Universal Distress Signal:

Three Puffs: To signal distress or emergency, create three distinct puffs of smoke. This pattern is universally recognized as a call for help.

Ensure Fire Safety:

Contain the Fire: Make sure your fire is contained within a safe area, like a fire ring or pit, to prevent it from spreading.

Monitor the Fire: Always keep an eye on the fire to ensure it doesn't get out of control. Never leave it unattended.

By learning how to create and use smoke signals, you can communicate effectively over long distances and in situations where other methods might not work.

Making Ground-to-Air Signals

Ground-to-air signals are crucial tools for getting noticed by rescuers and aircraft in emergencies. They are designed to communicate important messages from the ground, ensuring that help arrives when you need it most. Let's dive into how you can make and use these signals effectively!

The Purpose of Ground-to-Air Signals

Visibility and Communication:

- **Visibility from the Air:** Ground-to-air signals are large, visible symbols or patterns that can be easily seen by aircraft or rescuers flying overhead.
- **International Distress Symbols:** These signals use internationally recognized codes to communicate urgent messages, such as requests for assistance or confirmation of messages.

> ## Standard Ground-to-Air Signal Codes
>
> **The "X" Symbol:**
>
> - **Meaning:** This symbol indicates that you require assistance.
> - **How to Make It:** Arrange large rocks, branches, or use brightly colored materials to form a large "X" shape on the ground.
>
> **The "Y" Symbol:**
>
> - **Meaning:** This symbol means "Yes."
> - **How to Make It:** Lay out materials to create a large "Y" shape. This can be useful for answering questions or confirming information.
>
> **The "N" Symbol:**
>
> - **Meaning:** This symbol means "No."
> - **How to Make It:** Create a large "N" on the ground using rocks, branches, or other materials.

Materials Needed for Creating Ground-to-Air Signals

1. **Large Rocks, Branches, or Tarps:**
    - **Purpose:** These items help create the visible symbols.
    - **Types:** Gather large rocks, sturdy branches, or use large tarps to form the shapes.

2. **Brightly Colored Clothing or Materials:**
    - **Purpose:** Increases the visibility of the signals.
    - **Types:** Use bright fabrics or materials like orange, red, or yellow clothing, or any other vivid items you have.

3. **An Open, Flat Area:**
    - **Purpose:** Ensures that the signals are clear and visible from the air.
    - **Types:** Choose a clear, open space like a field or a large clearing.

Step-by-Step Instructions for Making Ground-to-Air Signals

1. **Choose the Right Location:**
    - Find an Open Area: Select a flat, open space where your signal will be visible from the air. Avoid areas with heavy vegetation or obstacles.

2. **Arrange Materials to Form Symbols:**
    - **Create the Symbol:** Lay out your materials (rocks, branches, or bright clothing) to form the chosen symbol. Make sure the symbol is large and clear.

3. **Maintain the Signal:**
   - **Keep It Visible:** Regularly check and clear any debris that might cover or obscure your signal. Ensure that it remains visible and recognizable.

4. **Stay Near the Signal:**
   - **Be Ready for Rescue:** Stay close to your signal so you can quickly respond to any rescue efforts. This also helps ensure that you're easily found.

Tips for Effective Ground-to-Air Signaling

Contrast with the Environment:

High Visibility: Make sure your signal stands out against the surroundings. Use bright colors or materials that contrast with the natural environment.

Use Additional Signals:

Combine Methods: Enhance your visibility by using other signaling methods, such as flares or mirrors, alongside your ground-to-air signals.

Quiz:
Chapter 8 – Navigating and Signaling Skills

Short Answer Questions

1. What is the main purpose of a compass in navigation?

2. How should you hold a compass to get an accurate reading?

3. Describe the steps to take a bearing using a compass.

4. What can interfere with the accuracy of a compass reading?

5. How can you use the sun to determine direction during the day?

Multiple Choice Questions

1. What part of the compass points towards magnetic north?

a) The Rotating Bezel
b) The Direction of Travel Arrow
c) The Needle
d) The Baseplate

2. What should you do after aligning the compass needle with the north marking?

a) Start walking immediately
b) Rotate the bezel to find the bearing
c) Ignore the degree markings
d) Change the compass direction

3. Which constellation can help you find true north in the northern hemisphere?

a) The Southern Cross
b) Orion's Belt
c) The Big Dipper
d) The Milky Way

4. In the southern hemisphere, which method helps you find north using an analog watch?

a) Point the hour hand at the sun
b) Point the 12 o'clock mark at the sun
c) Use the watch's second hand
d) Align the minute hand with the sun

5. Why is it important to combine solar navigation with other techniques?

a) To make the navigation process faster
b) To have a backup method in case one fails
c) To reduce the need for practice
d) To avoid using a map or compass

True or False Questions

1. The needle of a compass always points to magnetic north. (True/False)

2. You should avoid using metal objects near a compass to prevent interference. (True/False)

3. In the northern hemisphere, the midpoint between the hour hand and the 12 o'clock mark on an analog watch points to true north. (True/False)

4. The sun rises in the west and sets in the east. (True/False)

5. Using natural landmarks is an unreliable method for navigation because they can easily move. (True/False)

Chapter 9
Weather Prediction

The ability to predict the weather is an important skill for any outdoor adventure, as it allows you to anticipate and prepare for changing conditions. Mastering this skill enables you to plan your journey more effectively, avoid potential hazards, and make informed decisions that can enhance your safety

Weather Prediction: Observing Cloud Patterns

Understanding how to predict the weather by observing clouds is a valuable skill. Clouds can give us clues about upcoming weather conditions, from sunny days to storms. Let's dive into how you can use clouds to make weather predictions!

Different Types of Clouds and Their Significance

Cumulus Clouds:

- **Appearance:** Fluffy, white clouds with a puffy, cotton-like appearance.
- **Weather Indication:** Generally associated with fair weather. These clouds often mean the weather will be nice and sunny.

Stratus Clouds:

- **Appearance:** Low, gray clouds that cover the sky like a blanket, creating an overcast appearance.
- **Weather Indication:** These clouds often signal overcast conditions and can bring light rain or drizzle.

Cirrus Clouds:

- **Appearance:** High-altitude clouds that are thin, wispy, and sometimes look like delicate streaks across the sky.
- **Weather Indication:** Usually indicate fair weather, but they can signal that the weather is changing. They often appear before a change in the weather, like a storm or rain.

Nimbus Clouds:

- **Appearance:** Dark, thick clouds that cover the sky and can look heavy and ominous.
- **Weather Indication:** These are rain clouds and often bring storms or heavy rain. The darker and denser the cloud, the more likely it is to rain or storm.

Cloud Movement and Weather Changes

1. **Fast-Moving Clouds:**

    - **Observation:** If clouds are moving quickly across the sky, it might mean that the weather is changing. This could signal that a storm or weather front is approaching.

2. **Clouds Moving from the West:**

    - **Observation:** In many places, weather systems move from west to east. So, if clouds are moving in from the west, be prepared for changes in the weather.

3. **Clouds Forming and Dissipating Quickly:**

    - **Observation:** When clouds appear and disappear quickly, it might indicate unstable weather conditions. This can mean sudden changes, like a quick rain shower.

How to Observe Cloud Formations Over Time

1. **Keep a Weather Journal:**
    - **Activity**: Create a weather journal and note the types of clouds you see each day and the weather that follows. This helps you learn how different clouds are linked to weather changes.

2. **Take Photos of the Sky:**
    - **Activity:** Take pictures of the sky at different times of the day. Compare these photos to your weather journal to see how cloud patterns change over time.

3. **Compare Observations with Weather Forecasts:**
    - **Activity:** Check weather forecasts and compare them to your observations. This helps you understand how accurate your cloud predictions are.

Special Cloud Formations and What They Mean

1. **Anvil-Shaped Cumulonimbus Clouds:**
    - **Appearance:** These clouds have a distinctive anvil shape and are very tall. They often look dark and dense.
    - **Weather Indication**: These clouds can signal severe storms, including lightning, hail, and heavy rain.

2. **Lenticular Clouds:**
    - **Appearance:** Lens-shaped clouds that often form over mountains and can look like a stack of plates.
    - **Weather Indication:** Lenticular clouds often indicate strong winds and can signal turbulence or gusty conditions.

3. **Mammatus Clouds:**
    - **Appearance:** These clouds have a bulbous or pouch-like appearance and can follow severe thunderstorms.
    - **Weather Indication:** Mammatus clouds often appear after severe weather, and their presence can mean that more storms might be coming.

By learning to observe and interpret cloud patterns, you can become better at predicting the weather. Practice looking at the sky and using these tips to understand what the clouds are telling you about the weather!

Reading Animal Behavior: How Animals Can Help Predict the Weather

Animals have a unique ability to sense changes in the environment before we even notice them. By learning to read animal behavior, you can get clues about upcoming weather changes.

How Animals Sense Weather Changes

Animals are often more sensitive to environmental changes than we are. They can detect shifts in temperature, humidity, and air pressure that signal changes in the weather.

Here's how different animals react:

Birds Flying Low or Seeking Shelter:

- **Behavior:** Birds might fly lower to the ground or seek shelter when a storm is approaching.
- **Why:** Low-flying birds often seek refuge as they sense a drop in air pressure and humidity, which usually precedes bad weather.

Insects Becoming More Active:

- **Behavior:** Insects like flies and mosquitoes might become more active when the weather is fair.
- **Why:** Insects are often more active in warm, dry conditions. Increased activity can signal pleasant weather.

Livestock Behavior:

- **Behavior:** Animals such as cows and horses may lie down or seek shelter when rain is on the way.
- **Why:** Livestock can sense changes in atmospheric pressure and will often prepare for rain by resting or seeking cover.

Observing Bird Behavior for Weather Clues

Swallows Flying Low:

- **Observation:** Swallows might fly closer to the ground when the air is humid.
- **Weather Clue:** This behavior can indicate that rain is on the way because the insects they feed on are flying lower due to high humidity.

Seagulls Moving Inland:

- **Observation:** Coastal birds like seagulls might move inland before a storm.
- **Weather Clue:** This behavior can signal that a storm is approaching or that there will be strong winds.

Birds Falling Silent:

- **Observation:** Birds might stop singing or become very quiet.
- **Weather Clue:** A sudden quietness among birds can be a sign that a storm or severe weather is imminent.

Insects and Amphibians as Weather Indicators

Crickets Chirping More Frequently:

- **Observation:** Crickets chirp more often in warm weather.
- **Weather Clue:** Increased chirping can be a sign of warm weather and can sometimes be used to predict temperature changes.

Frogs Becoming More Vocal:

- **Observation:** Frogs might croak more during humid conditions.
- **Weather Clue:** Frogs are more active in humid weather, so increased croaking can signal rain or wet conditions.

Ants Building Higher Mounds:

- **Observation:** Ants may build their mounds higher or seal them off before a rainstorm.
- **Weather Clue:** Ants prepare for rain to protect their nests, so this behavior can indicate that rain is coming.

Tips for Monitoring Animal Behavior

Keep a Weather Journal:

Activity: Start a journal where you record animal behavior and the weather. Note how animals behave on different days and compare it to the weather conditions.

Purpose: This will help you see patterns and improve your ability to predict the weather based on animal activity.

Observe Your Pets:

Activity: Pay attention to your pets, such as dogs or cats. Pets often become restless or anxious before storms.

Purpose: Noting these changes can give you clues about approaching weather.

Watch Wildlife in Natural Areas:

Activity: Spend time observing animals in parks or natural areas. Look for patterns in how they behave in relation to the weather.

Using Wind and Temperature Changes: Predicting Weather with Nature's Clues

Wind and temperature are powerful indicators of upcoming weather changes. By learning to observe and interpret these natural signs, you can make educated guesses about what type of weather will soon be coming your way.

Understanding Wind Direction and Weather Conditions

1. **Winds from the West:**

    - **Observation:** If you notice the wind coming from the west, it often means that weather systems are moving your way.
    - **Weather Clue:** In many places, weather systems move from west to east. So, west winds might bring changes like rain or shifting weather.

2. **Winds from the East:**

    - **Observation:** Winds coming from the east can sometimes indicate unusual weather patterns or storms.
    - **Weather Clue:** In some regions, east winds can bring in stormy weather or sudden changes, as they often signal the arrival of low-pressure systems.

3. **Sudden Changes in Wind Direction:**

    - **Observation:** A sudden shift in wind direction can be a sign that weather fronts are moving in.
    - **Weather Clue:** These shifts can precede changes like thunderstorms or cooler weather, as different air masses collide.

How Wind Speed Affects Weather Predictions

1. **Calm Winds:**
   - **Observation:** Light or calm winds often accompany stable, fair weather.
   - **Weather Clue:** If the air is still and there's no noticeable breeze, it usually means the weather is stable and not changing quickly.

2. **Increasing Wind Speeds:**
   - **Observation:** If the wind starts to pick up, it might be a sign that storms or weather changes are approaching.
   - **Weather Clue:** Stronger winds can indicate the arrival of weather fronts, which might bring rain, snow, or storms.

3. **Gusty Winds:**
   - **Observation:** Sudden gusts or very strong winds can precede thunderstorms or cold fronts.
   - **Weather Clue:** Gusty winds often signal that a storm is near or that there will be significant weather changes.

Using Temperature Changes to Predict Weather

1. **Rapid Temperature Drops:**
   - **Observation:** If the temperature drops quickly, it could mean a cold front is moving in.
   - **Weather Clue:** Rapid cooling usually indicates that colder air is arriving, which might bring rain, snow, or stormy conditions.

2. **Gradual Warming:**
   - **Observation:** A gradual increase in temperature often suggests fair weather and high-pressure systems.
   - **Weather Clue:** When temperatures rise slowly, it often means stable, pleasant weather is expected.

3. **Temperature Differences Between Day and Night:**
   - **Observation:** Notice how temperature changes from day to night.
   - **Weather Clue:** Significant differences between daytime and nighttime temperatures can show that the weather is changing with the seasons or due to weather fronts.

Tips for Observing Wind and Temperature Changes

1. **Using a Simple Wind Vane:**
   - **Activity:** Make or use a wind vane to see which direction the wind is coming from.
   - **Purpose:** This helps you track wind patterns and understand how they relate to weather changes.

2. **Keeping a Thermometer Outside:**
   - **Activity:** Place a thermometer outside to monitor temperature changes throughout the day.
   - **Purpose:** Tracking temperature will help you recognize patterns and understand how temperature fluctuations relate to weather conditions.
3. **Recording Observations in a Weather Journal:**
   - **Activity:** Keep a journal where you write down wind directions, speeds, and temperature changes.
   - **Purpose:** Regularly recording these observations will help you identify trends and make more accurate weather predictions over time.

Putting Survival Skills To Practice Project: Weather Instruments

Making your own weather instruments is a fun and educational way to learn about meteorology and develop hands-on skills. By creating simple tools, you can measure and predict weather changes using materials you have at home.

DIY Weather Instruments: Why They're Cool

Creating weather instruments helps you:

- **Understand Basic Meteorological Principles:** Learn how air pressure, rainfall, and wind affect the weather.
- **Develop Hands-On Skills:** Gain practical experience by building and using your own tools.
- **Spark Curiosity About Weather:** Explore how different weather conditions can be measured and predicted.

Making a Simple Barometer

A barometer measures air pressure, which can help predict changes in the weather.

Materials Needed:

- A clear glass jar
- A balloon
- A drinking straw
- A piece of cardboard
- Tape or glue
- Scissors

Instructions:

1. **Prepare the Balloon:** Cut the balloon's neck off and stretch the remaining part over the opening of the jar. Secure it with a rubber band or tape. This will act as the flexible membrane of your barometer.
2. **Attach the Straw:** Tape or glue one end of the drinking straw to the center of the balloon. Make sure it's secure and horizontal. The straw will move up and down with changes in air pressure.

3. **Create a Scale:** Cut a piece of cardboard and place it next to the jar. Mark the position of the end of the straw at different times to record changes in air pressure. You can use these marks to observe how the straw's position changes with different weather conditions.

Interpreting Results:

- **High Pressure:** The straw will be in a lower position.
- **Low Pressure:** The straw will move up higher.

Making a Rain Gauge

A rain gauge measures the amount of rainfall. It's a great tool for tracking precipitation over time.

Materials Needed:

- A clear plastic bottle (with a screw cap)
- Scissors
- A ruler
- Permanent markers or tape
- A funnel (optional)

Instructions:

1. **Prepare the Bottle:** Cut the top off the plastic bottle just below the neck. You'll use the bottom part to collect rainwater.
2. **Mark the Measurements:** Use a ruler to measure and mark 1-inch intervals on the side of the bottle with permanent markers or tape. These marks will help you measure the amount of rainfall.
3. **Assemble the Rain Gauge:** Place the top part of the bottle (the funnel) upside down into the bottom part. This helps direct the rain into the bottle. If you don't have a funnel, just place the top part directly in the bottle.
4. **Position the Rain Gauge:** Place the rain gauge in an open area away from any obstructions like trees or buildings that might block the rain.

Recording Results:

- **Measure Rainfall:** After a rainstorm, check the water level in the gauge and note how much rain has collected. Compare your results to the markings to see how much rain fell.

Creating a Wind Vane and Anemomter

Wind Vane: Measures wind direction.

Materials Needed:

- A straw
- A piece of paper or cardboard
- A pin or thumbtack

- Scissors
- Glue or tape

Instructions:

1. **Prepare the Vane:** Cut a paper or cardboard into an arrow shape. Attach the arrow to the end of the straw using glue or tape.
2. **Assemble the Vane:** Poke a hole through the center of the straw and the end of a pencil or dowel. Insert a pin or thumbtack through the hole to allow the straw to spin freely.
3. **Position the Wind Vane:** Place the wind vane in an open area where it can catch the wind. The arrow will point into the wind, showing the direction from which it is coming.

Anemometer: Measures wind speed.

Materials Needed:

- Four plastic cups
- Straws
- A central pivot (like a pencil or dowel)
- Tape or glue

Instructions:

1. **Prepare the Cups:** Attach the cups to the ends of four straws, creating a cross shape with the straws.
2. **Assemble the Anemometer:** Secure the ends of the straws to the central pivot using tape or glue. Ensure the cups are positioned so they catch the wind.
3. **Position the Anemometer:** Place it in an open area where the wind can blow through the cups.

Observing Results:

- **Wind Vane:** Note the direction the arrow is pointing to understand the wind direction.
- **Anemometer:** Count how fast the cups spin to get an idea of the wind speed. Faster spinning means stronger winds.,

---

Final Tips

Practice Regularly: Observe your instruments frequently to get familiar with how they work.

Keep Records: Use a weather journal to track changes and patterns in the weather based on your instruments.

Have Fun Learning: Experiment with different designs and improvements to your weather tools.

Quiz:
Chapter 9 – Weather Predictions

Short Answer Questions

1. What type of cloud is fluffy and white with a cotton-like appearance, and usually indicates fair weather?
2. How can you use a weather journal to improve your ability to predict weather based on cloud patterns?
3. What behavior might you observe in birds if a storm is approaching?
4. What is a possible weather clue if you notice ants building their mounds higher before a rainstorm?
5. Describe what happens to the temperature when a cold front is moving in.

Multiple Choice Questions

1. Which type of cloud is associated with heavy rain and storms?

a) Cirrus
b) Cumulus
c) Nimbus
d) Stratus

2. If you notice the wind is coming from the west, what might this indicate?

a) Stable weather
b) Cold weather
c) Weather systems are moving your way
d) Warm weather

3. What should you do if you see birds flying low to the ground?

a) Expect sunny weather
b) Expect fair weather
c) Prepare for a storm
d) Prepare for cooler weather

4. Which type of cloud is thin and wispy, often indicating that weather might be changing?

a) Stratus
b) Cumulus
c) Cirrus
d) Nimbus

5. If you see a sudden increase in wind speed, what might this signal?

a) Calm weather
b) Weather fronts are moving in
c) Stable conditions
d) Fair weather

True or False Questions

1. Cumulus clouds are usually associated with stormy weather. (True/False)

2. An increase in cricket chirping is a sign of colder weather. (True/False)

3. The sun rising in the east and setting in the west is a good indication of where north and south are. (True/False)

4. Observing the behavior of insects can give you clues about upcoming weather changes. (True/False)

5. Rapid temperature increases generally suggest that a cold front is moving in. (True/False)

Chapter 10
Urban Survival Skills

The ability to predict the weather is an important skill for any outdoor adventure, as it allows you to anticipate and prepare for changing conditions. Mastering this skill enables you to plan your journey more effectively, avoid potential hazards, and make informed decisions that can enhance your safety

Avoiding Dangers – Staying Safe in Crowded Areas

1. **Importance of Situational Awareness**

Situational awareness means being alert and aware of your surroundings. It helps you recognize potential dangers and react quickly.

- **Scan the Environment Regularly:** Keep your eyes moving to notice changes or potential threats.
- **Identify Potential Exits:** Always be aware of where you can exit a crowded area quickly if needed.
- **Recognize Unusual Behavior:** Pay attention to people acting strangely or suspiciously. Trust your instincts and move away if something feels off.

2. **Strategies for Staying Safe in Crowded Places**

- **Stay Close to a Trusted Adult or Group:** It's easier to stay safe when you're with people you trust.
- **Have a Designated Meeting Point:** Agree on a spot to meet if you get separated from your group.
- **Avoid Pushing or Shoving:** Keep calm and move carefully to avoid accidents or injuries.

3. **Reacting in Emergency Situations**

- **Move Towards the Edges:** If you're in a crowd and something goes wrong, move to the edge to avoid being trapped.
- **Keep Low During a Fire:** If there's smoke, stay close to the ground where the air is clearer.
- **Use a Whistle or Loud Noise:** If you need help, a whistle or loud noise can attract attention.

4. **Keeping Personal Belongings Safe**

- **Keep Bags Zipped and Close:** Always zip up your bag and keep it close to your body.
- **Avoid Displaying Expensive Items:** Don't show off phones, jewelry, or other valuables.
- **Be Cautious of Bumps:** If someone bumps into you, be alert—it could be a pickpocket trying to steal from you.

Finding Safe Places in Urban Settings

1. **Importance of Identifying Safe Locations**

Knowing where to find safety can be crucial during emergencies. Safe locations are places where you can get help or protection.

- Shelter and Protection: Look for buildings or areas that can protect you from weather or danger.
- Access to Help: Safe places should have access to help or resources like food, water, and first aid.

2. **Identifying and Using Public Buildings**

- Libraries, Schools, and Community Centers: These places are often open to the public and can provide shelter and help.

- Police Stations and Fire Departments: These are official places where you can find emergency assistance.
- Hospitals and Medical Clinics: For medical emergencies, these are the best places to seek help.

3. **Recognizing Safe Spots in Less Obvious Places**

- Abandoned Buildings with Secure Entry: These can offer shelter but be cautious about the safety of the structure.
- Underground Shelters or Basements: In severe weather, these can offer protection from storms or floods.
- Rooftops or High Ground: For avoiding floods, high ground is a safe place to stay.

Staying Safe While Moving Through Urban

1. **Navigating the City Safely**

- **Stick to Well-Lit, Populated Areas**: Always choose paths that are well-lit and busy to stay safe.
- **Avoid Shortcuts Through Alleys:** These areas can be isolated and potentially dangerous.
- **Use Public Transportation Wisely:** Know your stops and routes to avoid getting lost or ending up in unsafe areas.

2. **Tips for Safe Transportation**

- Plan Your Route: Before you head out, know your route and how to get to your destination.
- Stay Aware on Public Transport: Keep your belongings secure and be mindful of your surroundings.

3. **Practice Makes Perfect**

- Explore Safely: Walk around your neighborhood or city to become familiar with safe places and routes.
- Discuss Safety with Adults: Talk about safety plans with your family so you're prepared for emergencies.

Remember, staying alert, being prepared, and knowing where to find help are key to navigating urban areas safely.

Quiz:

Chapter 10 – Urban Survival Skills

Short Answer Questions

1. What should you always be aware of in crowded areas to stay safe?
2. If you're in a crowded place and something goes wrong, where should you move to avoid being trapped?
3. What are two things you should do to keep your personal belongings safe in crowded areas?
4. Name one type of public building that can provide shelter and help in an emergency.
5. Why is it important to stick to well-lit and populated areas when navigating a city?

Multiple Choice Questions

1. What is a good strategy if you get separated from your group in a crowded place?

a) Wander around looking for them
b) Find a place to sit and wait
c) Go to a designated meeting point
d) Leave the area immediately

2. What should you do if you see someone acting strangely in a crowded area?

a) Ignore them and continue what you're doing
b) Approach them and ask if they need help
c) Trust your instincts and move away
d) Try to befriend them

3. If you need to get help in an emergency, what is a good method to attract attention?

a) Yell loudly
b) Use a whistle or loud noise
c) Wave your arms frantically
d) Use a flashlight

4. What is a safe spot in urban areas that is not a public building?

a) Abandoned buildings with secure entry
b) Dark alleys
c) Isolated rooftops
d) Busy sidewalks

True or False Questions

1. Cirrus clouds are usually a sign of heavy rain or storms. (True/False)

2. In a crowded area, you should always push through people to get out quickly. (True/False)

3. Libraries and community centers can provide shelter and assistance during emergencies. (True/False)

4. It is safer to take shortcuts through alleys when navigating the city. (True/False)

5. Keeping your bag unzipped in a crowded place is fine as long as you are alert. (True/False)

Chapter 11
Basic Self-Defense Techniques

Learning self-defense is not just about fighting; it's about knowing how to protect yourself and feeling confident in your ability to stay safe. Self-defense skills help you react effectively in dangerous situations, build your confidence, and reduce fear. By learning basic self-defense, you gain valuable tools that can help you feel more secure and in control.

Basic Self-Defense Moves

Here are some simple and effective self-defense techniques that are easy to remember and practice:

Blocking and Deflecting Attacks

- **How to Block:** If someone is trying to hit you, use your forearm to block their attack. Position your arm so that it intercepts their hand or object, and absorb the impact with your arm.
- **How to Deflect:** Use your hand to push away an incoming strike or object, redirecting it safely away from you. This can create a momentary break in the attacker's action.

Striking Vulnerable Areas

- **Eyes:** If you need to defend yourself, a quick jab to the eyes can cause temporary blindness and give you time to escape.
- **Nose:** A sharp, upward strike to the nose can be very painful and disorient the attacker.
- **Groin:** A powerful kick or strike to the groin can be highly effective and painful, giving you a chance to get away.

Using Everyday Objects as Defensive Tools

- **Keys:** Hold your keys between your fingers when you feel threatened, so they can be used to scratch or poke.
- **Books:** Use a book as a shield to block blows or as a heavy object to push away an attacker.

Using Self-Defense Responsibly

It's important to understand when and how to use self-defense techniques properly:

Only Use Self-Defense as a Last Resort

- Try to avoid physical confrontations whenever possible. Use your self-defense skills only if there is no other way to escape or seek help.

Avoid Escalation and Seek Help First

- If you can, talk calmly to de-escalate the situation. Seek help from trusted adults or authorities before resorting to self-defense.

Practicing De-Escalation Techniques

- **Calm Speaking:** Use a calm and firm voice to tell the person to stop or back away.
- **Creating Distance:** Move away from the situation if possible, keeping yourself safe without confrontation.

Tips for Staying Physically and Mentally Prepared

1. Take Self-Defense Classes

- Enroll in self-defense classes or workshops to learn and practice techniques with trained instructors.

2. Practice with a Trusted Adult or Friend

- Regularly practice self-defense moves with a trusted adult or friend to build confidence and improve your skills.

3. Stay Physically Fit

- Being in good physical shape helps you react more quickly and effectively. Engage in regular physical activities to maintain strength and agility.

By learning and practicing these basic self-defense techniques, you can feel more confident and prepared to handle difficult situations. Remember, the goal of self-defense is to protect yourself and get to safety, not to engage in fights or escalate conflicts. Stay safe, stay aware, and always use your skills responsibly.

Quiz:
Chapter 11 – Basic Self-Defense Techniques

Short Answer Questions

1. What should you use to block an incoming attack?

2. Name two vulnerable areas of the body that you can target in self-defense.

3. What is one way to use keys as a defensive tool?

4. When should you use self-defense techniques?

5. What is a good method for de-escalating a confrontation?

Multiple Choice Questions

1. What is the best way to use a book in self-defense?

a) As a weapon to hit the attacker
b) To shield yourself from blows or push away the attacker
c) To throw at the attacker
d) To block their vision

2. Which technique involves pushing away an object or strike to redirect it safely?

a) Blocking
b) Deflecting
c) Striking
d) Grabbing

3. What should you do if you find yourself in a dangerous situation?

a) Ignore the situation and walk away
b) Try to avoid physical confrontation and seek help
c) Engage in a fight immediately
d) Yell loudly at the attacker

4. Which of the following is NOT a recommended self-defense move?

a) Striking the groin
b) Jab to the eyes
c) Using a book as a shield
d) Shouting at the attacker

5. How can staying physically fit help with self-defense?

a) It improves your ability to run away quickly
b) It makes you stronger for hitting harder
c) It helps you stay calm during confrontations
d) It allows you to carry more self-defense tools

True or False Questions

1. You should use self-defense techniques as a first option in any dangerous situation. (True/False)

2. Holding your keys between your fingers can be used to scratch or poke an attacker. (True/False)

3. You should always try to de-escalate a confrontation before using self-defense. (True/False)

4. Practicing self-defense with a friend or trusted adult can help build confidence and improve skills. (True/False)

5. Regular physical activity is important for staying in shape and enhancing self-defense skills. (True/False)

Chapter 12
First Aid Essentials

Knowing basic first aid is an essential skill that helps you take care of yourself and others in emergencies.

Treating Cuts and Scrapes

1. **Cleaning and Disinfecting a Wound**

- **Step 1: Wash Your Hands**
  - Before you start treating any wound, wash your hands thoroughly with soap and water to prevent introducing germs to the wound.

- **Step 2: Clean the Wound**
  - Use clean water and mild soap to gently clean the wound. Rinse the area to remove any dirt or debris.

- **Step 3: Apply an Antiseptic**
  - After cleaning, apply an antiseptic solution to kill any remaining germs. This helps prevent infection.

2. **Bandaging a Wound**

- **Choosing the Right Bandage**
  - Select a bandage or gauze that fits the size of the wound. For small cuts, adhesive bandages are usually sufficient. For larger wounds, you'll need gauze and medical tape.

- **Applying Adhesive Bandages**
  - For small cuts, place the adhesive bandage directly over the wound. Make sure the bandage covers the entire area to keep it clean.

- **Using Gauze and Tape**
  - For larger wounds, place a piece of gauze over the wound and secure it with medical tape. Make sure the gauze is large enough to cover the wound and the tape is securely fastened.

3. **Monitoring for Infection**

- Signs of Infection
  - Redness and Swelling: If the area around the wound becomes red and swollen, it could be infected.
  - Pus or Unusual Discharge: Any yellow or green pus coming from the wound is a sign of infection.
  - Increasing Pain and Warmth: If the wound becomes more painful and feels warm to the touch, it might be infected.

Preventing Cuts and Scrapes

1. **Wearing Protective Clothing**
   - **During Outdoor Activities:** Always wear appropriate clothing like gloves and long sleeves when working with sharp tools or playing rough sports.
   - **When Using Sharp Objects:** Use tools and utensils carefully and follow safety instructions to avoid accidents.

2. **Being Cautious**
   - **Handling Sharp Objects:** Always handle knives, scissors, and other sharp tools with care. Cut away from your body and use these objects safely.
   - **Avoiding Rough Play:** Be mindful during playtime, especially on hard surfaces. Avoid games that might result in falls or injuries.

Dealing with Burns and Blisters

Burns and blisters can be painful and sometimes serious. Knowing how to treat them properly can make a big difference in recovery.

Understanding Burns

First-Degree Burns

- **What They Look Like:** Redness, minor pain, and swelling.
- **How to Treat:** Cool the burn with running water and cover it with a sterile bandage.

Second-Degree Burns

- **What They Look Like:** Blisters, intense pain, and swelling.
- **How to Treat:** Cool the burn with running water and protect it with a sterile, non-stick bandage. Do not pop the blisters.

Third-Degree Burns

- **What They Look Like:** White, charred, or leathery skin; severe pain or numbness.
- **What to Do:** Seek adult help immediately. Third-degree burns require professional medical treatment.

Treating Minor Burns

1. **Cooling the Burn**

- **Step 1: Rinse with Water**
  - Cool the burn under running lukewarm water for at least 10 minutes. This helps to reduce the heat and pain.

- **Step 2: Apply a Bandage**
  - After cooling, cover the burn with a sterile, non-stick bandage. Avoid using ice, butter, or oily substances, as they can make the burn worse.

2. **Avoiding Common Mistakes**

- No Ice or Butter
  - Don't apply ice or butter to burns. Ice can damage the skin further, and butter can cause infections.

- Don't Pop Blisters
  - If blisters form, leave them intact. Popping blisters can lead to infection.

Handling Blisters

Caring for Blisters

1. **Step 1: Clean the Area**
   - Gently clean the area around the blister with mild soap and water.
2. **Step 2: Protect with a Bandage**
   - Cover the blister with a blister pad or a clean bandage. This will protect it from further friction and injury.
3. **Avoid Popping**
   - Do not pop the blister. It acts as a natural barrier against infection.

When to Seek Adult Help

Signs of Serious Burns

- **Large Area Burns**
  - If the burn covers a large area of the body, seek help immediately.
- **Burns on Sensitive Areas**
  - Burns on the face, hands, feet, or genitals need professional care.
- **Signs of Shock**
  - Look for signs of shock, such as pale skin, rapid pulse, or shallow breathing. If these signs are present, get help right away.

Handling Sprains and Strains

Sprains and strains are common injuries that can happen during physical activities. Knowing the difference between them and how to treat them properly can help you recover faster and get back to doing what you love. This chapter will explain what sprains and strains are, how to treat them using the R.I.C.E. method, and when to seek help.

Understanding Sprains and Strains

Sprains

- What They Are: Sprains happen when the ligaments, which are the bands of tissue connecting bones at a joint, are stretched or torn. They commonly occur in the ankles, wrists, and knees.
- What It Feels Like: Pain, swelling, bruising, and difficulty moving the affected joint.

Strains

- What They Are: Strains occur when muscles or tendons (the tissues that connect muscles to bones) are stretched or torn. They often happen in the back, legs, or arms.
- What It Feels Like: Pain, muscle spasms, swelling, and difficulty moving the affected muscle.

Using the R.I.C.E. Method

The R.I.C.E. method is a simple way to treat sprains and strains and help them heal. Here's how to use it:

Rest

- What to Do: Stop using the injured area to prevent further damage. Rest is important for healing.
- How to Rest: Avoid activities that put weight or strain on the injured area. If it's a sprained ankle, try to keep off it as much as possible.

Ice

- What to Do: Apply ice to the injured area to reduce swelling and numb the pain.
- How to Ice: Wrap an ice pack or a bag of frozen vegetables in a cloth (to protect your skin) and apply it to the injury for 15-20 minutes every hour for the first 24 hours.

Compression

- What to Do: Use an elastic bandage to wrap the injured area and help reduce swelling.
- How to Compress: Wrap the bandage snugly but not too tight. You should be able to slide a finger under the bandage. Make sure the wrapping does not cut off circulation.

Elevation

- What to Do: Keep the injured limb elevated above the level of your heart to help reduce swelling.
- How to Elevate: Prop up the injured area on pillows or a cushion while sitting or lying down.

When to Seek Medical Help

Sometimes, sprains and strains can be more serious than they seem. You should get professional help if:

1. **Inability to Bear Weight**
   - If you can't put weight on the injured limb or it feels unstable, see a doctor.
2. **Severe Pain or Swelling**
   - If the pain or swelling doesn't improve after a few days, or it gets worse, seek medical attention.
3. **Numbness or Tingling**
   - If you experience numbness, tingling, or loss of movement in the injured area, it could be a sign of a more serious injury.

Preventing Sprains and Strains

1. **Warm Up**

   - **Why It's Important:** Warming up helps prepare your muscles and ligaments for physical activity and reduces the risk of injury.

   - **How to Warm Up:** Do gentle stretches and exercises before starting sports or activities.

2. **Wear Proper Footwear and Gear**

   - **Why It's Important:** Proper shoes and safety gear can help prevent injuries.

   - **What to Wear:** Choose shoes that fit well and provide good support, and wear appropriate gear for the activity.

3. **Avoid Uneven Surfaces and Risky Movements**

   - **Why It's Important:** Uneven surfaces and risky movements can increase the chance of injury.

   - **What to Do:** Be cautious on uneven ground and avoid sudden, awkward movements.

Recognizing and Treating Dehydration

Water is essential for keeping our bodies healthy and functioning properly. It helps regulate body temperature, transport nutrients, and keep our organs working. Staying hydrated is especially important when you're active, during hot weather, or when you're feeling unwell.

Why Water is Essential

Functions of Water in the Body

- **Temperature Regulation:** Water helps your body stay cool by sweating and breathing out moisture.
- **Nutrient Transport:** It carries nutrients to your cells and helps remove waste from your body.
- **Joint Lubrication:** Water keeps your joints lubricated, which helps you move smoothly.

Daily Water Intake Recommendations

- How Much to Drink: Kids typically need about 6-8 cups (1.5-2 liters) of water a day. This can vary based on age, activity level, and climate.

Signs and Symptoms of Dehydration

Recognizing when you or someone else is dehydrated is crucial for staying healthy. Here's what to look out for:

1. **Dry Mouth and Throat**
    - **What It Feels Like:** Your mouth and throat might feel dry or sticky.

2. **Dizziness or Lightheadedness**
    - **What It Feels Like:** You might feel unsteady or like you're going to faint.

3. **Dark Yellow Urine**
    - **What It Looks Like:** Urine that is darker than usual can be a sign of dehydration. Healthy urine should be light yellow.

Steps for Treating Mild to Moderate Dehydration

1. **Drink Small Sips of Water Frequently**
    - **What to Do:** Sip water slowly throughout the day rather than drinking a lot at once. This helps your body absorb it better.

2. **Use Oral Rehydration Solutions (ORS) if Available**
    - **What It Is:** ORS is a special solution that helps replace lost fluids and electrolytes. You can find it in pharmacies or make a simple version at home (1/2 teaspoon of salt and 6 teaspoons of sugar mixed in 1 liter of water).

3. **Eat Water-Rich Foods**
    - **What to Eat:** Fruits and vegetables like watermelon, cucumbers, and oranges contain a lot of water and can help with hydration.

When to Seek Help for Severe Dehydration

Severe dehydration can be dangerous and requires immediate attention. Get help if you notice these serious symptoms:

1. **Persistent Vomiting or Diarrhea**
    - **What to Do:** If vomiting or diarrhea doesn't stop, seek medical help immediately.
2. **Extreme Thirst and Dry Skin**
    - **What It Feels Like:** Extreme thirst and very dry, cool skin can be signs of severe dehydration.
3. **Confusion or Lethargy**
    - **What to Do:** If someone seems unusually confused, sleepy, or unresponsive, get help right away.

Tips for Staying Hydrated

1. Carry a Water Bottle

Why It Helps: Having water with you makes it easier to drink regularly.

2. Drink Before You Feel Thirsty

Why It Helps: Don't wait until you're thirsty to drink. Regular sipping prevents dehydration.

3. Be Mindful of Activity and Weather

What to Do: Drink more water when you're playing sports or on hot days.

Recognizing and Treating Frostbite and Hypothermia

When temperatures drop, it's important to know how to protect yourself from frostbite and hypothermia. Both conditions are serious and require quick action to prevent harm.

Understanding Frostbite and Hypothermia

1. **What is Frostbite?**
    - **Definition:** Frostbite is an injury caused by freezing of the skin and underlying tissues. It most commonly affects the fingers, toes, nose, and ears.
    - **What Happens:** When exposed to cold temperatures, the blood vessels in your extremities constrict, reducing blood flow and causing tissues to freeze.
2. **What is Hypothermia?**
    - **Definition:** Hypothermia occurs when your body loses heat faster than it can produce it, causing your core temperature to drop to dangerously low levels.
    - **What Happens:** Prolonged exposure to cold weather can overwhelm your body's ability to stay warm, leading to a drop in body temperature.

Recognizing Frostbite

1. **Early Signs of Frostbite**
    - **Red or Pale Skin:** Skin may look pale or waxy.
    - **Numbness or Tingling:** Affected areas might feel numb or tingly.

2. **Advanced Signs of Frostbite**
   - **Blisters:** Blisters may form on the skin, and the area may become hard and swollen.
   - **Skin Color Changes:** Skin can turn blue or gray and may feel cold and hard.

Treating Frostbite

1. **Get to a Warm Place**
   - **What to Do:** Move indoors or to a sheltered area as soon as possible to prevent further exposure.
2. **Warm the Affected Areas Slowly**
   - **How to Do It:** Use warm (not hot) water to gently warm the frostbitten areas. Soak them for about 30 minutes, or until feeling returns.
   - **Avoid:** Never use direct heat like a stove, heating pad, or hot water, as it can cause burns.
3. **Avoid Rubbing or Massaging the Area**
   - **Why:** Rubbing can cause more damage to frozen tissues.
4. **Seek Medical Attention**
   - **When:** If frostbite is severe or if the affected areas don't improve, get professional medical help immediately.

Recognizing Hypothermia

1. **Early Signs of Hypothermia**
   - **Shivering:** Shivering is an early sign that your body is trying to generate heat.
   - **Cold Skin:** Skin may feel cold and appear pale.
2. **Advanced Signs of Hypothermia**
   - **Confusion or Drowsiness:** You might feel confused, sleepy, or have trouble speaking.
   - **Slurred Speech:** Difficulty speaking or moving may occur.
   - **Weak Pulse:** A weak or irregular pulse can be a sign of severe hypothermia.

Treating Hypothermia

1. **Get to a Warm Place**
   - **What to Do:** Move indoors or to a warm, sheltered area immediately.
2. **Warm the Person Gradually**
   - **How to Do It:** Use blankets, warm clothing, or warm (not hot) water bottles to gradually increase body temperature. Avoid rapid warming techniques, as they can be dangerous.
3. **Offer Warm Drinks**
   - **What to Provide:** Give warm (not hot) drinks like tea or hot chocolate to help warm the body from the inside.

4. **Avoid Sudden Movements**
   - **Why:** Sudden movements can put additional strain on the heart and lead to complications.
5. **Seek Medical Help**
   - **When:** If symptoms are severe or if the person doesn't improve with home treatment, get professional medical help right away.

Preventing Frostbite and Hypothermia

1. **Dress Appropriately**
   - **What to Wear:** Wear layered clothing, including thermal underwear, insulated jackets, hats, gloves, and waterproof boots. Avoid cotton, as it retains moisture and can increase the risk of frostbite.
2. **Stay Dry**
   - **Why:** Wet clothing can accelerate heat loss. Make sure to stay dry by avoiding snow or rain and changing wet clothes promptly.
3. **Take Breaks**
   - **What to Do:** Take regular breaks in a warm place if you're spending time outdoors in cold weather.
4. **Be Mindful of Weather Conditions**
   - **Why:** Check weather forecasts and avoid going outside in extremely cold or windy conditions if possible.

Nature's First Aid Kit – 25 Most Common Plants, Roots, Bark, and Berries

Imagine you're out exploring the woods, and suddenly, you scrape your knee or feel a sting from an insect bite. What if you could find something in nature that could help? The wild is full of amazing plants, roots, bark, and berries that can be used to make simple first aid remedies.

1. **Aloe Vera (Aloe vera)**

- **Found:** In warm climates, especially in dry, sandy areas.
- **Use:** The gel inside the leaves can be applied to burns, cuts, and insect bites for soothing relief.

2. **Yarrow (Achillea millefolium)**

- **Found:** Meadows, roadsides, and open fields.
- **Use:** Crushed leaves can be applied to wounds to help stop bleeding. It can also be used to reduce swelling.

3. **Plantain (Plantago major)**

- **Found:** Lawns, gardens, and along trails.
- **Use:** The leaves can be crushed and applied to insect bites, stings, and small cuts to reduce itching and promote healing.

4. **Echinacea (Echinacea purpurea)**

- **Found:** Meadows and prairies.
- **Use:** Chew on the root to help boost your immune system and fight off colds or infections.

5. **Comfrey (Symphytum officinale)**

- **Found:** Damp, grassy places like riverbanks.
- **Use:** Crushed leaves can be made into a paste to help heal bruises, sprains, and broken bones. Do not use comfrey on deep wounds.

6. **Burdock Root (Arctium lappa)**

- **Found:** Fields, roadsides, and waste areas.
- **Use:** The root can be crushed and used as a poultice to draw out infections from wounds.

7. **Chickweed (Stellaria media)**

- **Found:** Gardens, fields, and shady areas.
- **Use:** Crushed leaves can be used to soothe itchy skin or rashes.

8. **Wild Rose (Rosa spp.)**

- **Found:** Forest edges, meadows, and hedgerows.
- **Use:** The petals can be made into a soothing tea for sore throats, and the hips (fruit) are full of vitamin C.

9. **St. John's Wort (Hypericum perforatum)**

- **Found:** Meadows and sunny areas.
- **Use:** The leaves and flowers can be crushed and applied to scrapes and burns to help heal the skin.

10. **Elderberry (Sambucus nigra)**

- **Found:** Along streams and in moist woodlands.
- **Use:** The berries can be made into a syrup to boost the immune system and help fight off colds.

11. **Slippery Elm Bark (Ulmus rubra)**

- **Found:** In forests, especially near water.
- **Use:** The inner bark can be chewed or made into a tea to soothe sore throats and coughs.

12. **Mullein (Verbascum thapsus)**

- **Found:** Fields and roadsides.
- **Use:** The leaves can be used to make a tea to help with coughs, and the flowers can be used in oil to treat earaches.

13. **Dandelion (Taraxacum officinale)**

- **Found:** Almost everywhere, from lawns to meadows.

- **Use:** The leaves can be used to reduce inflammation, and the roots can be made into a tea to help with digestion.

14. **Pine (Pinus spp.)**
- **Found:** Forests and woodlands.
- **Use:** The inner bark can be chewed or made into a tea for a boost of vitamins, especially vitamin C.

15. **Blackberry (Rubus fruticosus)**
- **Found:** In hedgerows, fields, and forests.
- **Use:** The leaves can be chewed or made into a tea to help with diarrhea and sore throats.

16. **Willow Bark (Salix spp.)**
- **Found:** Near streams, lakes, and wetlands.
- **Use:** The bark can be chewed or made into a tea to relieve pain, similar to how aspirin works.

17. **Chamomile (Matricaria chamomilla)**
- **Found:** Fields and gardens.
- **Use:** The flowers can be made into a calming tea that helps with stomach aches and helps you relax.

18. **Goldenrod (Solidago spp.)**
- **Found:** Meadows, fields, and roadsides.
- **Use:** The flowers can be used to make a tea that helps with allergies and colds.

19. **Calendula (Calendula officinalis)**
- **Found:** Gardens and meadows.
- **Use:** The petals can be made into a salve to help heal cuts, scrapes, and burns.

20. **Red Clover (Trifolium pratense)**
- **Found:** Fields, meadows, and along roadsides.
- **Use:** The flowers can be used to make a tea that helps with coughs and colds.

21. **Mint (Mentha spp.)**
- **Found:** Gardens, fields, and near water.
- **Use:** The leaves can be chewed or made into a tea to soothe an upset stomach or cool a fever.

22. **Peppermint (Mentha piperita)**
- **Found:** Gardens and near streams.
- **Use:** The leaves can be used in a tea to help with headaches, digestion, and muscle aches.

23. **Jewelweed (Impatiens capensis)**
- **Found:** Wet, shaded areas like riverbanks.

- **Use:** The leaves can be crushed and applied to skin to soothe poison ivy, stings, and rashes.

24. Catnip (Nepeta cataria)

- **Found:** Fields, gardens, and along roadsides.
- **Use:** The leaves can be made into a tea to help you relax and get a good night's sleep.

25. Garlic (Allium sativum)

  - **Found:** Gardens and wild in some areas.
  - **Use:** The cloves can be crushed and applied to wounds to help prevent infections or eaten to boost the immune system.

Quiz:

Chapter 12 – First Aid Essentials

Short Answer Questions

1. What is the first step you should take before treating any wound?

2. How should you treat a first-degree burn?

3. What are two signs of infection in a wound?

4. When should you seek adult help for a burn?

5. What does the acronym R.I.C.E. stand for in treating sprains and strains?

Multiple Choice Questions

1. What is the proper way to clean a wound?

a) Use only a dry cloth
b) Rinse with clean water and mild soap
c) Apply ice directly
d) Cover with butter

2. What should you use to cover a small cut or scrape?

a) Gauze and tape
b) Adhesive bandage
c) Ice pack
d) Oily substance

3. What is a common mistake to avoid when treating burns?

a) Using lukewarm water
b) Applying a sterile bandage
c) Applying ice or butter
d) Seeking help for severe burns

4. What type of burn involves blisters and requires a non-stick bandage for protection?

a) First-degree burn
b) Second-degree burn
c) Third-degree burn
d) Fourth-degree burn

5. When handling a blister, what should you do to protect it?

a) Pop the blister to drain it
b) Apply a blister pad or clean bandage
c) Leave it uncovered
d) Apply butter to soothe it

True or False Questions

1. You should use antiseptic solution on a wound after cleaning it. (True/False)

2. It's okay to apply ice directly to a burn. (True/False)

3. When treating a sprain, you should avoid using the affected joint and follow the R.I.C.E. method. (True/False)

4. Blisters should be popped to relieve pain and prevent infection. (True/False)

5. You should seek adult help if a burn covers a large area or is on sensitive parts of the body. (True/False)

Chapter 13
Interactive Learning and Practice

Imagine spending an exciting and challenging weekend with your family in the great outdoors, learning how to build shelters, start fires, and find your way using a compass. A family survival weekend is not only an exciting adventure but also an opportunity to practice essential survival skills in a fun and safe way.

This is a special event where your family spends time together, away from screens and the distractions of everyday life, to focus on learning and practicing survival skills. Whether you're in a local park, your backyard, or a camping site, the goal is to work together as a team, build communication skills, and strengthen family bonds through shared self-reliance experiences.

Benefits of a Family Survival Weekend

Building Teamwork and Communication Skills:

- During a survival weekend, every member of the family has a role to play. Whether it's gathering materials for a shelter, starting a campfire, or navigating with a compass, working together to achieve common goals helps everyone learn how to communicate and cooperate more effectively.

Strengthening Family Bonds Through Shared Experiences:

- There's something special about facing challenges together as a family. The memories you create while building a shelter, cooking a meal over a fire, or figuring out how to purify water will stay with you for a lifetime. These shared experiences bring families closer and create lasting bonds.

Creating a Safe Environment for Skill Practice:

- A family survival weekend is the perfect opportunity to practice survival skills in a controlled, safe environment. With everyone together, you can experiment, make mistakes, and learn from them without the pressure of a real survival situation.

Planning Your Family Survival Weekend

Now that you understand the benefits (and all out fun!) of a family survival weekend, it's time to plan your own adventure. Here's a step-by-step guide to help you get started.

1. **Selecting a Suitable Location:**

   - **Backyard:** If it's your first time, starting in your own backyard is a great idea. It's convenient, familiar, and you can still experience the outdoors.
   - **Local Park:** For a bit more of a challenge, choose a local park with woods, trails, and open spaces. Make sure to check the rules and regulations before setting up camp.

- **Camping Site:** If your family is ready for a more immersive experience, head to a camping site. Look for one that allows you to practice skills like fire-building and shelter construction.

2. **Preparing a List of Essential Gear and Supplies:**
   - **Shelter:** Tent, tarp, ropes, and stakes.
   - **Fire:** Matches, lighters, fire starters, and kindling.
   - **Food and Cooking:** Non-perishable foods, portable stove, cooking utensils, pots, and pans.
   - **Navigation:** Compass, maps, and GPS (as a backup).
   - **Water:** Water bottles, purification tablets, and a water filter.
   - **Safety:** First aid kit, sunscreen, insect repellent, and flashlights.
   - **Clothing:** Weather-appropriate clothing, hats, gloves, and sturdy shoes.
   - **Tools:** Knife, multitool, shovel, and saw.
   - **Other:** Sleeping bags, blankets, notebooks, and pens.

3. **Setting Clear Objectives and Activities for the Weekend:**
   - Decide on the skills you want to practice, such as shelter building, fire starting, navigation, and water purification.
   - Create a schedule that includes time for each activity, meals, and breaks.
   - Make sure everyone in the family understands the objectives and what's expected of them during each activity.

Specific Survival Challenges to Include

To make sure your family survival weekend offers both a good time and skill building, here are some specific challenges you can include:

1. **Building a Family Shelter Using Natural Materials:**
   - **Objective:** Work together to build a shelter using only natural materials like branches, leaves, and vines.
   - **Instructions:** Find a suitable location for your shelter, gather materials, and construct a simple lean-to or debris hut. Make sure it's sturdy and provides enough protection from the elements.

2. **Starting a Campfire and Cooking a Meal Together:**
   - **Objective:** Learn how to safely start a campfire and cook a meal over it.
   - **Instructions:** Gather firewood, kindling, and tinder. Practice different fire-starting methods, such as using matches or a fire starter. Once the fire is going, cook a simple meal like hot dogs, marshmallows, or foil-wrapped vegetables.

3. **Navigating a Predetermined Route Using a Compass:**
   - **Objective:** Practice using a compass to navigate a route.
   - **Instructions:** Choose a route in your location and mark waypoints. Give each family member a turn at navigating to the next point using a compass. Discuss how to read a map and orient yourself in the wilderness.

4. **Conducting a Water Purification Exercise:**
   - **Objective:** Learn how to purify water from a natural source.
   - **Instructions:** Find a nearby stream or lake and collect water. Demonstrate how to use a water filter, purification tablets, or boiling to make the water safe to drink. Discuss the importance of clean water in a survival situation.

Reflect, Review, and Ready for Next Time

After spending a weekend practicing survival skills with your family, the adventure doesn't end when you return home. One of the most important parts of the experience is reflecting on what you've learned and discussing it together. This section guides you through the process of debriefing, sharing your experiences, and setting goals for future survival practice. These activities will help you understand what went well, identify areas for improvement, and ensure that your next survival adventure is even better.

The Importance of Debriefing and Reflection

Debriefing is a time for everyone to sit down together and talk about the weekend. It's a chance to review what you did, how you did it, and what you learned. Reflection helps you think about your experiences, understand what worked well, and figure out what could be improved. This process is important because it helps you and your family learn from your experiences and become even more prepared for future survival situations.

Discussing What Went Well and What Could Be Improved

Start your debrief by discussing what went well during the weekend. Here are some questions to guide your conversation:

- What activities were the most fun? Talk about the challenges you enjoyed the most, like building a shelter or starting a fire.

- What skills did we do well? Identify the skills that everyone picked up quickly and did well, such as navigating with a compass or cooking over a campfire.

- What did we find challenging? Discuss any activities that were difficult or didn't go as planned. For example, did you have trouble keeping the fire going, or did your shelter not turn out as sturdy as you hoped?

- Next, think about what could be improved:

- What could we do differently next time? Talk about how you can improve the activities that were challenging. Maybe you need to practice fire-starting more or learn more about shelter-building techniques.

- Did we have the right gear and supplies? Review the gear and supplies you brought. Was there anything you wish you had, or something you didn't need? This will help you better prepare for the next survival weekend.

Sharing Individual Experiences and Insights

Everyone in the family will have their own unique experiences and insights from the weekend. Take time for each person to share what they learned:

- What was your favorite part of the weekend? Everyone should share their favorite activity or moment. It might be something they learned, a challenge they overcame, or just a fun moment with the family.

- What did you learn about yourself? Encourage everyone to think about what they discovered about themselves during the weekend. Did they learn they're good at problem-solving, or that they need to work on staying calm in challenging situations?

- How did we work together as a team? Reflect on how well the family communicated and worked together. What did you do well as a team, and how can you improve your teamwork in the future?

Setting Goals for Future Survival Practice

Finally, use what you've learned to set goals for future survival practice. These goals will help you focus on improving your skills and preparing for the next adventure:

- Which skills do we want to practice more? Identify the skills that need more practice. Maybe you want to get better at fire-starting, shelter-building, or water purification.
- What new skills do we want to learn? Think about what new survival skills you want to learn as a family. This could be anything from advanced navigation techniques to learning how to fish or trap small game.
- When can we have our next survival weekend? Plan your next family survival weekend! Set a date and start thinking about what new challenges you can include to m make it even more exciting and educational.

Building Shelters and Fires

You don't have to go far into the wilderness to practice important survival skills—your own backyard can be the perfect place! Practicing survival skills at home offers a safe and convenient way to learn and grow.

The Benefits of Practicing Survival Skills at Home

Practicing survival skills in your backyard has several benefits that make it an ideal starting point for learning:

1. **Easy Access to Resources and Supervision:**
    - Your backyard provides easy access to all the materials you need, like branches, leaves, and tarps. Plus, practicing at home means there's always an adult nearby to supervise and help out if needed.
2. **Opportunities for Regular and Consistent Practice:**
    - Since your backyard is just steps away, you can practice survival skills regularly. Whether it's after school, on the weekends, or during a break, you have the chance to keep improving your skills whenever you want.
3. **Creating a Controlled Environment for Experimentation:**
    - Your backyard offers a controlled environment where you can experiment with new techniques and ideas. You can try different ways to build shelters or start a fire, and if something doesn't work, it's easy to adjust and try again.

Step-by-Step Instructions for Backyard Shelter Building

Building shelters is one of the most important survival skills, and you can practice it right in your backyard. Here are some easy shelters you can build:

Lean-to Shelter Using Garden Branches and Leaves:

- Materials Needed: Long branches, leaves, and a sturdy tree or fence.
    - **Instructions:**
        1. Find a strong tree or fence to act as the main support for your shelter.
        2. Lean long branches against the tree or fence at an angle, creating the basic frame.

3. Cover the frame with leaves, grass, or other natural materials to provide insulation and protection from the wind.
4. Make sure the shelter is stable and that there's enough space inside for you to sit or lie down.

Tarp Shelter with Ropes and Stakes:

- **Materials Needed:** Tarp, rope, stakes, and a few rocks or logs.
  - **Instructions:**
    1. Find two sturdy trees or poles in your backyard.
    2. Tie a rope between the trees, about waist-high.
    3. Drape the tarp over the rope to create a sloping roof.
    4. Secure the tarp's edges to the ground using stakes, rocks, or logs to keep it in place.
    5. Adjust the tarp to make sure it's tight and can withstand wind or rain.

Debris Hut Using Raked Leaves and Grass:

- **Materials Needed:** Lots of raked leaves, grass, and small branches.
  - **Instructions:**
    1. Create a small frame using branches, similar to a teepee shape.
    2. Pile raked leaves and grass over the frame, making sure to cover it completely.
    3. Add more leaves and grass until the walls are thick and insulated.
    4. Leave a small opening as an entrance, and check that the shelter is sturdy and cozy inside.

How to Safely Start a Fire in the Backyard

Learning how to start a fire is a key survival skill, but it's important to do it safely. Here's how you can practice fire-starting in your backyard:

Using a Fire Pit or Fire-Safe Container:

- **Materials Needed:** Fire pit, metal container, matches or flint and steel, kindling, and small sticks.
  - **Instructions:**
    1. Set up a fire pit or use a fire-safe container in a clear area of your backyard, away from trees, bushes, and buildings.
    2. Gather kindling (small twigs, dry leaves, and pine needles) and small sticks.
    3. Create a small pile of kindling in the center of the fire pit or container.
    4. Practice using matches or flint and steel to start the fire. Make sure an adult is there to supervise.
    5. Once the kindling catches fire, slowly add small sticks to build up the fire.
    6. Always have a bucket of water or sand nearby to extinguish the fire if needed.

Practicing Different Fire-Starting Methods:

- **Matches:** Hold the match close to the kindling and strike it away from your body. Lightly blow on the flame to help it grow.
- **Flint and Steel:** Strike the steel against the flint to create sparks. Aim the sparks at the kindling until it catches fire.

Emphasizing Fire Safety Rules and Adult Supervision:

Never leave a fire unattended.

Always have an adult present when starting or tending a fire.

Make sure the fire is completely out before leaving the area.

Additional Backyard Survival Activities

1. **Creating a Backyard Obstacle Course to Test Physical Fitness:**
   - Set up an obstacle course using items like logs, ropes, and tires. Practice climbing, crawling, and balancing to build strength and agility.

2. **Setting Up a Mock Campsite with Tents and Cooking Gear:**
   - Practice setting up a tent, laying out sleeping bags, and organizing your campsite. You can also cook a simple meal using a portable stove or over your backyard fire.

3. **Practicing First Aid Scenarios with Family Members:**
   - Use your backyard to practice first aid skills, like bandaging wounds, treating burns, or handling sprains. Have family members act out different scenarios so you can practice what to do in an emergency.

Scavenger Hunts for Edible Plants

Scavenger hunts aren't just a game—they're a fantastic way to learn about the natural world, especially when it comes to identifying edible plants. Scavenger hunts offer a unique way to learn by turning exploration into a game. Here's why they're so valuable:

Making Learning Fun and Interactive:

- Scavenger hunts turn the process of learning into a game, which makes it more enjoyable. Instead of just reading about plants, you get to go out and find them, which makes the experience much more engaging.

Encouraging Observation and Exploration:

- By searching for specific plants, you'll learn to observe the details around you more closely. Whether it's the shape of a leaf, the color of a berry, or the texture of bark, you'll start noticing things you might have missed before.

Providing Hands-On Experience with Plant Foraging:

- Scavenger hunts give you real-life experience with identifying and foraging for edible plants. This hands-on practice helps you remember what you've learned and gives you the confidence to identify plants on your own.

Guidelines for Organizing a Scavenger Hunt

Ready to organize your own scavenger hunt? Follow these steps to make sure it's a success:

1. **Creating a List of Common Edible Plants to Find:**
   - Start by making a list of edible plants that are common in your area. Include plants that are easy to identify and safe for beginners, like dandelions, clover, or wild strawberries. You can also include pictures or descriptions to help with identification.

2. **Choosing a Safe and Accessible Location:**
   - Pick a location that's safe and easy to access, like a local park, garden, or even your backyard. Make sure it's a place where the plants on your list are likely to be found. Always have an adult with you to supervise and ensure safety.

3. **Setting Clear Rules and Objectives for the Hunt:**
   - Before you start, set some ground rules. For example, explain that everyone should only pick a small amount of each plant to avoid over-harvesting. Set objectives for the hunt, like finding a certain number of plants or identifying specific characteristics of each one.

Ways to Make the Scavenger Hunt Engaging

A scavenger hunt is already fun, but you can make it even more exciting with these ideas:

Adding Clues and Riddles Related to Plant Characteristics:

- Create clues or riddles that describe the plants on your list. For example, you might write, "I have a bright yellow flower and fluffy seeds that float away on the breeze—what am I?" This adds an extra challenge and helps reinforce plant identification skills.

Timing the Hunt to Add a Competitive Element:

- Set a time limit for the scavenger hunt to add some friendly competition. See who can find the most plants in the shortest amount of time, or who can identify a rare plant first.

Offering Small Rewards or Incentives for Successful Identification:

- Encourage participation by offering small rewards for correctly identifying plants. This could be anything from stickers to a special treat. The goal is to make learning fun and rewarding.

The Importance of Reviewing and Discussing Findings

After the scavenger hunt, take some time to review what you found. This reflection is key to reinforcing what you've learned:

Comparing Collected Plants with Identification Guides:

- Lay out all the plants you have found and compare them with an identification guide or the pictures on your list. This helps confirm whether you identified the plants correctly and teaches you to spot differences between similar species.

Discussing the Uses and Benefits of Each Plant:

- Talk about the different uses of each plant. For example, some plants might be edible, while others have medicinal properties. Understanding the benefits of each plant adds to your knowledge and appreciation of the natural world.

Emphasizing the Importance of Sustainable and Safe Foraging:

- It's important to remember that foraging should always be done sustainably. Discuss why it's crucial to only take what you need and to leave enough behind so the plant can continue to grow. Also, always make sure a plant is safe to eat before trying it.

Navigation Exercises – Compass and Map Challenges

Knowing how to navigate using a compass and a map is a critical survival skill. It's not just about finding your way; it's about building confidence, developing problem-solving abilities, and learning to think critically in unfamiliar situations.

Understanding how to read a map and use a compass isn't just something you learn in a book—real mastery comes from practice. Here's why:

1. **Reinforcing Theoretical Knowledge Through Practical Application:**
   - Reading about navigation is one thing, but actually using a map and compass in the field helps you understand and remember the concepts much better. Hands-on practice turns theory into real skills.

2. **Building Confidence in Navigating Unfamiliar Terrain:**
   - The more you practice navigating, the more confident you'll become in finding your way, even in places you've never been before. This confidence is crucial in survival situations.

3. **Developing Problem-Solving and Critical Thinking Skills:**
   - Navigation exercises force you to think critically and solve problems on the go. Whether it's figuring out the best route or adjusting to unexpected obstacles, you'll learn to make smart decisions quickly.

Step-by-Step Instructions for Setting Up Navigation Exercises

Ready to practice your navigation skills? Here's how to set up your own navigation exercises:

1. **Creating a Simple Map of the Practice Area:**
   - Start by choosing a safe and familiar area like your backyard or a local park. Draw a simple map of the area, marking important features like trees, rocks, or buildings. This map doesn't need to be perfect—just clear enough to help you practice.

2. **Setting Up Waypoints and Checkpoints for the Navigation Course:**
   - Next, choose a few spots in your practice area to be your waypoints or checkpoints. These are places you'll navigate to using your map and compass. Mark them on your map and place something noticeable at each spot, like a flag or a small marker.

3. **Preparing Compasses and Other Navigation Tools:**
   - Make sure you have a compass for each person taking part in the exercise. You might also want to bring a notebook and pencil to jot down notes or draw extra sketches. If you have a GPS device, you can use it to check your accuracy but try to rely on your compass and map as much as possible.

How to Use a Compass and Map Together

Now that your course is set up, it's time to learn how to use your map and compass together:

1. **Orienting the Map with the Compass:**
   - The first step in using a map and compass together is to orient the map. This means lining up the map so that it matches the real world around you. To do this, place the compass on the map and rotate the map until the compass needle points north. Now your map is aligned with the terrain.

2. **Taking Bearings and Plotting Routes:**
   - A bearing is the direction you need to travel to reach a specific point. To take a bearing, hold the compass flat and point it toward your destination. Read the degree number where the compass needle lines up. Now, you can use this bearing to guide your path. Mark your route on the map and follow it carefully.

3. **Recognizing and Using Natural Landmarks for Guidance:**
   - As you navigate, look for natural landmarks like trees, hills, or streams that match features on your map. These landmarks help confirm that you're on the right path and can guide you if you get off course.

Additional Navigation Challenges

Once you've got the basics down, try these challenges to improve your skills:

1. **Setting Up a Treasure Hunt with Hidden Items at Each Waypoint:**
   - Turn your navigation exercise into a treasure hunt! Hide small items or notes at each waypoint and use your map and compass to find them. This adds an element of fun and gives you a goal to work toward.

2. **Creating a Timed Navigation Course to Test Speed and Accuracy:**
   - For a bit of competition, set a timer and see how quickly you can complete the course. You can challenge yourself to beat your own time or compete with friends and family to see who can navigate the fastest and most accurately.

3. **Practicing Nighttime Navigation with Reflective Markers:**
   - For an added challenge, try navigating at night using reflective markers. This will test your ability to rely on your compass and map without the help of daylight. Remember to stay safe and have an adult supervise nighttime activities.

True Survival Stories – Kids Who Made It

The Night in the Wilderness: Boy Survives Alone

Story: In a dense forest in Utah, 9-year-old Dylan Powell found himself lost after becoming separated from his family during a camping trip. With the temperature dropping and night falling, Dylan remembered the survival skills his dad had taught him. He quickly gathered sticks and leaves to build a makeshift shelter and huddled inside to stay warm. Dylan's ability to remain calm and use his knowledge of shelter-building kept him safe until rescuers found him the next day.

Key Skills: Dylan's survival hinged on his ability to stay calm and think clearly. Building a shelter protected him from the cold, and his knowledge of the outdoors helped him survive until help arrived.

Inspiration: Dylan's story highlights how important it is to practice survival skills like shelter-building. Knowing what to do in a difficult situation can make all the difference.

First Aid Hero: Girl Saves Friend After a Fall

Story: When 12-year-old Rebecca Carlisle's friend fell from a tree during a hike in the mountains of Colorado, she knew she had to act fast. Her friend had a deep cut on her leg and was bleeding heavily. Rebecca used the first aid skills she learned in her scout troop to stop the bleeding by applying pressure and elevating the injured leg. She stayed with her friend, keeping her calm, until rescuers arrived.

Key Skills: Rebecca's quick thinking and first aid knowledge saved her friend's life. By stopping the bleeding and keeping her friend calm, she prevented the situation from getting worse.

Inspiration: This story shows the importance of learning basic first aid. Knowing how to respond in an emergency can be the difference between life and death.

Lost but Not Hopeless: Siblings Navigate to Safety

Story: Siblings Caroline and Jackson Harris, aged 13 and 10, were hiking in the Smoky Mountains when they lost their way after taking a wrong turn. As night approached, they realized they were in serious trouble. Remembering their father's lessons, they decided to stay put and use natural landmarks like the position of the sun and the direction of river flow to determine their location. The next morning, they used these landmarks to navigate their way back to a trail and were found by park rangers.

Key Skills: Caroline and Jackson's knowledge of navigation and their decision to stay put overnight were crucial to their survival. They used the natural environment to help them find their way back.

Inspiration: This story emphasizes the value of understanding basic navigation skills and the importance of staying calm and using what you know to make smart decisions.

Trapped in a Snowstorm: Teen Survives by Building a Snow Cave

Story: When 15-year-old Michael Mason found himself caught in a sudden snowstorm while skiing in the Rockies, he knew he had to act quickly. The snow was piling up fast, and he couldn't find his way back. Remembering a lesson from his outdoor survival class, Michael dug a snow cave to shelter himself from the wind and cold. He hunkered down inside, conserving his energy, and waited out the storm. After two days, rescuers found him alive and well.

Key Skills: Michael's knowledge of building a snow cave saved him from hypothermia. His decision to conserve energy and stay sheltered in the snow cave until rescue was vital to his survival.

Inspiration: Michael's story shows the importance of learning specific survival techniques, like building a snow shelter. These skills can be lifesaving in extreme conditions.

> The stories of these young survivors teach us that bravery, resourcefulness, and knowledge can help anyone—even kids—overcome the toughest challenges. By practicing survival skills and staying calm in difficult situations, you too can be prepared to handle whatever comes your way. Remember, survival isn't just about strength; it's about using your mind and skills to stay safe and find your way back to safety.

Learning from Mistakes – What Not to Do

When you're out in the wilderness, it's important to make good decisions to stay safe. However, mistakes can happen, and they can turn a fun adventure into a dangerous situation. Let's take a look at some common mistakes kids have made in survival situations and learn what we can do to avoid them. These stories will help you understand why safety and preparedness are so important when you're out in nature.

Lost and Alone – Staying with Your Group

What Happened: Tommy was on a camping trip with his scout group. He was having a great time exploring the woods. One afternoon, while the group was hiking, Tommy spotted a cool bird and decided to follow it. He wandered off the trail, thinking he could catch up with his group later. But after a while, he realized he was lost. The trees all looked the same, and he couldn't find his way back. Panic set in as the day got darker, and Tommy didn't know what to do.

Consequences: Because Tommy didn't stay with his group, he got lost in the woods. This made it much harder for the group to find him, and he spent several hours alone, scared, and cold before he was finally rescued.

Lesson Learned: Always stay with your group, especially in unfamiliar areas. If you need to leave for any reason, tell someone where you're going and make sure they know how long you'll be gone. If you do get separated, stay where you are so that rescuers can find you more easily.

The Danger of Untreated Water – Drinking Safely

What Happened: Lily was out on a hike with her family when they ran out of water. It was a hot day, and Lily was very thirsty. She saw a clear, cool stream and, without thinking, drank some of the water. It tasted fine, so she drank even more. A few days later, Lily started feeling really sick. Her stomach hurt, and she was nauseous. She had caught a nasty illness from drinking untreated water.

Consequences: Drinking untreated water can expose you to harmful bacteria and parasites that can make you very sick. In Lily's case, she had to visit the doctor and missed a week of school while she recovered.

Lesson Learned: Never drink water straight from lakes, rivers, or streams without treating it first. You can purify water by boiling it, using a water filter, or adding purification tablets. Always carry enough clean water with you on hikes, and know how to purify water in case you need to use a natural source.

The Fire that Got Out of Control – Fire Safety

What Happened: Jake was excited to build his first campfire during a family camping trip. He had seen his dad do it before and thought he knew what to do. But Jake didn't clear the area around the fire pit, and he used too much dry wood and leaves. The fire quickly grew larger than he expected, and a gust of wind blew embers into the nearby bushes. The bushes caught fire, and soon there was a small wildfire. Jake's parents had to act fast to put it out, but it was a scary situation for everyone.

Consequences: A fire that gets out of control can cause serious damage to the environment and put lives at risk. In Jake's case, the fire could have spread further and endangered their entire campsite and the forest.

Lesson Learned: When building a fire, always follow proper safety rules. Clear the area around your fire pit of leaves, sticks, and other flammable materials. Keep your fire small and manageable, and never leave it unattended. Always have water or sand nearby to put out the fire if it starts to spread.

Ignoring the Weather – The Storm that Came

What Happened: Sara was camping with her friends when she noticed that the sky was getting darker and the wind was picking up. She heard distant thunder but thought it was far away. Her friends wanted to keep playing by the lake, and she didn't want to miss out, so she ignored the warning signs. Before long, the storm was upon them, and they were caught in heavy rain and lightning. They had to run back to their tents, soaked and shivering, and the temperature dropped quickly. Sara ended up with a mild case of hypothermia because she got too cold and wet.

Consequences: Ignoring weather signs can lead to dangerous situations like being caught in a storm, which can result in injury or illness. Sara's hypothermia could have been much worse if they hadn't gotten warm and dry quickly.

Lesson Learned: Always pay attention to the weather. If you notice signs of an approaching storm, like dark clouds, a sudden drop in temperature, or distant thunder, it's time to seek shelter. Staying dry and warm is crucial in preventing hypothermia. It's better to be safe and head back early than to risk getting caught in dangerous weather.

The Importance of Safety and Preparedness

These stories show how easily a fun adventure can turn into a dangerous situation if you're not careful. Here are some key takeaways to help you stay safe:

- Stay with Your Group: Never wander off alone, and always let someone know where you're going.
- Purify Water: Always treat water from natural sources before drinking it.

- Follow Fire Safety Rules: Clear the area around your fire, keep it small, and never leave it unattended.
- Watch the Weather: Pay attention to weather signs and seek shelter if a storm is coming.

Finally, always double-check your gear and supplies before heading out, and practice your survival skills regularly. The more prepared you are, the more confident and capable you'll be in any situation. Remember, learning from mistakes—whether your own or someone else's—is a powerful way to improve your skills and stay safe in the great outdoors.

Continuous Learning – How to Keep Improving Your Skills

Survival skills are not just something you learn once and then forget about. Like any important skill, they get better the more you practice them. Continuous learning and regular practice help you stay prepared, confident, and ready for anything that comes your way. It is essential that you keep practicing your survival skills, how you can make practice part of your everyday life, and how you can track your progress and learn from others.

The Power of Practice: Why Keep Learning?

When you practice your survival skills regularly, you're not just remembering what to do—you're building muscle memory and instinctive reactions. This means that in a real survival situation, you'll be able to act quickly and correctly, even under pressure. Here are some benefits of continuous learning:

- **Building Muscle Memory:** Repeating skills like tying knots, starting a fire, or setting up a shelter helps your body remember the motions. This way, when you need to do them in a hurry, you won't have to think too hard about it—you'll just know how.
- **Staying Prepared:** Life is full of surprises, and you never know when you might need your survival skills. By practicing regularly, you'll be ready for unexpected situations, whether it's a surprise storm during a hike or a power outage at home.
- **Increasing Confidence and Self-Reliance:** The more you practice, the more confident you'll feel in your abilities. This confidence makes you more self-reliant, meaning you'll be able to take care of yourself and others if something goes wrong.

Everyday Practice: How to Keep Your Skills Sharp

You don't need to wait for a big camping trip to practice your survival skills. There are plenty of ways to incorporate them into your everyday life. Here are some fun and practical ideas:

- **Backyard Camping:** Set up a tent in your backyard and spend a night outdoors. Practice building a small campfire (with adult supervision) and cooking a simple meal over it, like roasting marshmallows or heating up soup.
- **Outdoor Clubs or Scouting Groups:** Joining a group like Scouts or an outdoor club can give you regular opportunities to practice your skills. These groups often have activities like hiking, camping, and learning new survival techniques.
- **Educational Videos and Survival Books:** Watching videos or reading books about survival can teach you new skills and reinforce what you already know. Try out what you learn in a safe environment, like your backyard or a local park.

- **Homeschool Lessons:** If you are part of a homeschooling family, incorporate self-reliance and vocational skills training into your curriculum. Life skills definitely hold an important place in the education of young people. Programs like The Homestead Homeschool and The Tuttle Twins are excellent examples of ways to incorporate self-reliance skill building into your home learning day.

Tracking Your Progress: Keeping a Survival Skills Journal

One of the best ways to keep improving is by tracking your progress. A survival skills journal is a great tool to help you do this. Here's how to start:

- **Take Notes:** Write down the skills you're practicing, what you did well, and what you found challenging. This will help you see your progress over time and identify areas where you can improve.

- **Reflect on Your Successes and Challenges:** After each practice session, take a moment to reflect. What did you learn? What would you do differently next time? This reflection helps you learn from your experiences and get better each time.

- **Set New Goals:** Challenge yourself to learn new skills or improve the ones you already know. Maybe you want to learn how to build a different type of shelter or get faster at starting a fire. Setting goals keeps you motivated and focused on continuous improvement.

Learning from Others: Finding Mentors and Resources

You're not alone in your survival skills journey—there are lots of people who can help you learn and grow. Here's how to connect with them:

- **Workshops and Classes:** Look for survival skills workshops or classes in your community. These are often taught by experts who can show you new techniques and give you personalized tips. Go with your family to survival events like the Heritage Skills USA, Heritage Explorers, or Prepper Camp events where you all can engage in hands-on learning with a whole new community of like-minded folks from around the country.

- **Family Members:** If you have family members who are experienced in the outdoors, ask them to teach you what they know. Spending time together learning survival skills can be a fun and valuable experience.

- **Online Communities:** There are many online forums and communities where people share tips, advice, and experiences about survival skills. Joining one of these communities can help you learn from others and stay inspired to keep improving.

Keep Learning, Keep Growing

Continuous learning is the key to becoming really good at survival skills. By practicing regularly, tracking your progress, and learning from others, you'll keep getting better and better. Remember, the more you learn, the more confident and prepared you'll be for whatever challenges come your way. Keep practicing, stay curious, and always be ready to learn something new.

Fun and Safe Survival Games to Play with Friends

Learning survival skills doesn't have to be all about serious practice. It can be just outright fun too! One of the best ways to get better at survival skills is by playing games that let you practice while having a blast with your friends. These exciting survival-themed games will help you learn, work as a team, and solve problems—all while having a great time.

Why Play Survival Games?

Survival games combine learning with play, making it easier and more enjoyable to practice important skills. Here's why they're so awesome:

- **Reinforce Skills Through Play:** Games make it fun to practice skills like fire-starting, shelter-building, and navigation. The more you play, the better you get!

- **Teamwork and Problem-Solving:** Many survival games require you to work together with friends, solving problems and making decisions as a team.

- **Engaging and Enjoyable:** When learning is fun, you're more likely to stick with it. Survival games turn practice into an exciting adventure.

Survival Games You Can Play

Here are some specific games you can play with your friends to practice your survival skills. Each game is designed to be fun, educational, and safe.

Scavenger Hunt for Survival Items

Objective: Find and collect a list of survival items or natural resources within a certain area.

How to Play:

- Create a list of items that would be useful in a survival situation. This can include things like dry wood, rocks for a fire ring, leaves for shelter, or even items like water bottles and rope.

- Set a time limit (like 30 minutes) and see who can find and collect the most items from the list.

- You can play this game in your backyard, at a park, or in a safe wooded area.

Learning Focus: Identifying and gathering resources quickly.

Timed Shelter-Building Challenge

Objective: Build a small shelter using only the materials you find around you.

How to Play:

- Divide into teams or play individually. Each team gets a set amount of time (like 20 minutes) to build the best shelter they can using natural materials like branches, leaves, and rocks.

- After the time is up, test each shelter by seeing how well it protects from the wind or holds together.

Learning Focus: Shelter-building techniques and creativity.

Fire-Starting Races

Objective: Be the first to start a small fire using different methods.

How to Play:

- Gather different fire-starting tools like matches, flint and steel, or a magnifying glass. Make sure to have plenty of safe tinder, like dry leaves or cotton balls.
- Set up safe, small fire pits or areas for each player or team.
- Start the race and see who can get a fire going first (with adult supervision, of course!).

Learning Focus: Fire-starting techniques and patience.

Navigation Challenges

Objective: Use a map and compass to navigate to different checkpoints.

How to Play:

- Set up a series of checkpoints in a park or large backyard. Each checkpoint should be marked on a map, and you should use a compass to find them.
- Players or teams must navigate from one checkpoint to the next, either racing against the clock or against each other.
- The first team to reach all the checkpoints wins.

Learning Focus: Map reading, compass use, and orienteering.

Safety First: Setting Rules for Survival Games

While these games are meant to be fun, it's important to play safely. Here's how to ensure everyone stays safe while having a great time:

Adult Supervision: Always have an adult nearby when playing survival games, especially those involving fire or outdoor exploration.

Safe Areas: Choose safe, familiar places like your backyard, a local park, or a designated camping area to play. Avoid areas with real dangers, like steep cliffs, deep water, or dense forests.

Mock Scenarios: Use pretend or mock scenarios for your games. For example, don't use real knives or sharp tools, and always use safety equipment when necessary.

Get Creative: Inventing Your Own Games

The best part about survival games is that you can get creative and make up your own! Here are some tips for creating new games:

- **Unique Challenges:** Think about the skills you've learned and create challenges based on them. Maybe you set up an obstacle course that requires you to use different survival skills along the way.

- **Themed Adventures:** Add a storyline to your game, like pretending you're lost in the wilderness and need to find your way back to camp. This makes the game even more exciting!

- **Group Activities:** Invite friends, family, or neighbors to join in. The more people, the more fun—and the more you'll learn from each other.

Playing to Learn

By combining play with practice, you'll get better at survival techniques without even realizing it. Plus, you'll build teamwork, problem-solving abilities, and confidence along the way. So, gather your friends, set up some challenges, and start playing your way to becoming a survival expert!

Quiz:
Chapter 13 – Interactive Learning and Practice

Short Answer Questions

1. What are two benefits of having a family survival weekend?

2. Name one place where you can have a family survival weekend if you're looking for a bit more of a challenge than your backyard.

3. What should you include in your essential gear for a family survival weekend? Name at least two items.

4. What is the purpose of debriefing after a family survival weekend?

5. List two specific survival challenges you could include in your family survival weekend.

Multiple Choice Questions

1. Which of the following is a suitable location for a beginner family survival weekend?

a) Desert
b) Your backyard
c) A deserted island
d) A city downtown

2. What is the first step in safely starting a fire in your backyard?

a) Gather kindling and small sticks
b) Light the fire with matches
c) Use a fire pit or fire-safe container
d) Leave the fire unattended

3. What should you do if you are practicing fire-starting and the kindling catches fire?

a) Add large logs immediately
b) Make sure an adult is supervising
c) Pour water on it to make it go out
d) Ignore it and walk away

4. When building a shelter using natural materials, what should you use to cover the frame of a lean-to shelter?

a) Plastic sheets
b) Leaves, grass, or other natural materials
c) Old clothes
d) Metal sheets

5. What is one thing you should discuss during the debriefing after a family survival weekend?

a) The latest movies
b) What went well and what could be improved
c) Favorite TV shows
d) What video games to play next

True or False Questions

1. A family survival weekend can help build teamwork and communication skills. (True/False)

2. It's okay to use ice or butter on a burn during a survival practice. (True/False)

3. You should always have an adult present when starting or tending a fire. (True/False)

4. Creating a scavenger hunt for edible plants can be a fun and educational activity. (True/False)

5. During the debriefing, you should only talk about the things that went well and not discuss any challenges faced. (True/False)

Final thoughts for young adventurers

Congratulations! You've reached the end of the book, and that means you've taken an important step in learning essential survival skills. The purpose of this book was to equip you with the knowledge, confidence, and resilience you need to handle unexpected situations—whether you're in the great outdoors or just dealing with challenges in everyday life. By now, you should feel more prepared to face whatever comes your way, knowing that you have the skills and mindset to overcome obstacles.

Recap: What We've Learned

Let's take a moment to recap the key points we've covered in each chapter of this book:

1. Understanding the Basics of Survival

We learned about the most important survival priorities: finding shelter, water, fire, and food. You now know why these are crucial and how to approach each one in a survival situation.

2. Shelter Building

You explored different types of shelters and practiced building them using natural materials. We talked about how to stay safe and warm, and why shelter is often your first priority.

3. Finding and Purifying Water

This chapter taught you how to find water in the wild and purify it so it's safe to drink. You learned about different purification methods, like boiling, filtering, and using purification tablets.

4. Fire Starting Techniques

You discovered several ways to start a fire, from using matches to creating sparks with flint and steel. We also covered fire safety and how to keep your fire under control.

5. Navigation Skills

In this chapter, you learned how to use a map and compass to find your way. We discussed how to read natural signs to navigate and the importance of always knowing where you are.

6. Understanding Basic First Aid

We covered the basics of treating common injuries like cuts, burns, sprains, and insect bites. You learned how to clean wounds, apply bandages, and make splints using materials you have on hand. This chapter also emphasized the importance of carrying a well-stocked first aid kit whenever you go out into nature. We discussed the essential items to include and how to use them effectively.

7. Foraging for Wild Foods

You discovered how to identify safe, edible plants in the wild and the importance of knowing which plants to avoid. We talked about how to recognize different types of edible plants, berries, and nuts. This chapter also taught you how to responsibly harvest wild foods without harming the environment. You also learned simple ways to prepare what you've foraged, whether it's roasting nuts or making a simple salad from wild greens. We stressed the importance of never eating anything you can't positively identify as safe. The chapter also covered how to test new foods in small amounts and what to do if you experience an adverse reaction.

8. **Continuous Learning**

We emphasized the importance of practicing your survival skills regularly and keeping a survival journal to track your progress. This chapter was all about how to keep improving.

9. **Fun and Safe Survival Games**

You discovered that learning survival skills can be fun by playing survival-themed games with your friends. We shared some cool games that help you practice while having a great time.

10. **Learning from Mistakes**

We talked about common mistakes made in survival situations and what you can learn from them. The focus was on understanding what not to do and how to avoid dangerous situations.

11. **Safety and Preparedness**

We covered the importance of being prepared before heading out on any adventure. You learned about packing the right gear, checking the weather, and letting someone know your plans.

Key Takeaways

Here are the essential lessons and skills you should have gained from this book:

1. **Confidence:** You now have the knowledge and skills to handle unexpected situations, which gives you the confidence to stay calm and think clearly.

2. **Resilience:** Learning survival skills teaches you to be resourceful and resilient, helping you bounce back from challenges.

3. **Preparedness Mindset:** You understand the importance of being prepared, whether that means packing the right gear or practicing your skills regularly.

4. **Safety:** Above all, you've learned how to stay safe in different situations, from building a shelter, to starting a fire, and navigating through the wilderness. In both first aid and foraging, safety is key. Always think before you act, and make sure you're taking steps to protect yourself and others.

5. **Be Prepared:** Always carry a first aid kit and know how to use it. Understanding basic first aid can help you and others stay safe and healthy in the wild.

6. **Know Your Surroundings:** Learn to identify the plants around you so you can safely forage for food in nature. This knowledge not only helps you survive but also connects you to the environment.

Your Next Steps

Now that you've learned so much, it's time to take action:

1. **Practice Regularly:** Keep practicing the skills you've learned so they become second nature. Try new challenges, set goals, and track your progress in your survival journal.

2. **Stay Curious:** Never stop learning! There's always more to discover about survival skills. Read more books, watch videos, and try out new techniques.

3. **Share Your Knowledge:** Teach your friends and family what you've learned. Not only does this reinforce your own skills, but it also helps others stay safe and prepared.

4. **Embrace Adventure:** Get outside, explore nature, and put your skills to the test in safe, controlled environments. The more you practice in real-life situations, the more confident you'll become.

5. **Build Your First Aid Kit:** If you haven't already, gather the supplies for your own first aid kit. Make sure it's ready to go on your next adventure.

6. **Get Foraging:** With a trusted adult, start identifying plants in your local area. Practice safely harvesting and preparing wild foods, beginning with the plants you know are safe.

Final Encouragement

You've done something incredible by learning these survival skills. Remember, you are capable and prepared to face challenges with confidence and resilience. Life is full of surprises, but with the knowledge and skills you've gained, you can handle whatever comes your way.

Keep embracing the spirit of adventure, stay curious, and always be ready to learn and grow. The world is full of amazing experiences waiting for you—so get out there, explore, and enjoy every moment. You're ready for anything! You've come a long way in your journey through this book, learning skills that could one day make a big difference. The purpose of this book has always been clear: to equip you with essential survival skills that build your confidence, resilience, and knowledge so that you're prepared for unexpected situations. Whether you find yourself lost in the wilderness or simply want to feel more self-reliant, these skills will help you stay safe and confident.

A Note From The Author

Thank you for embarking on this journey through Ultimate Survival & Wilderness Skills for Kids! I hope that the skills and knowledge shared in these pages inspire you and the young adventurers in your life to feel prepared, confident, and resilient, no matter what challenges may come your way. Teaching children survival skills is not just about readiness; it's about building self-confidence, problem-solving abilities, and an appreciation for nature.

If you enjoyed the book, I would be so grateful if you could leave a review. Your feedback helps spread the word, making it easier for other parents, educators, and young readers to discover and benefit from this guide. Reviews mean the world to authors, and your support helps ensure that more kids can learn these valuable skills.

QR CODE

Thank you again for reading, and may your future adventures be safe and filled with wonder!

Warm regards,

WYATT CARSON

Survival Skills Quiz Answers

Chapter 1 Quiz Answer Key:

1. Importance of learning survival skills.

b) To build confidence and become a problem-solver

2. An outcome of learning survival skills.

b) A problem-solver

3. Additional learning besides practical skills.

c) How to face unexpected challenges with confidence

4. Getting lost on a family hike.

c) Stay calm, assess your situation, and think about what survival skills you can use

5. Not a basic safety rule for survival situations.

b) Approach and feed wild animals

6. Importance of telling an adult your plans.

b) So they know where to find you if something goes wrong

7. What to do if you see dark clouds and strong winds.

b) Seek shelter immediately

8. Staying calm in a survival situation.

b) It helps you think clearly and make better decisions

9. Making yourself more visible to rescuers.

c) Use bright clothing or reflective items to signal your location

10. Not a survival skill mentioned in this chapter.

d) Cooking a meal on a campfire

Chapter 2 Quiz Answer Key:

1. Importance of water.

b) It helps regulate temperature, keeps organs working, and flushes out toxins

2. The number of days your body can survive without water.

b) 3 days

3. A sign of dehydration.

b) Dark yellow urine

4. The safest way to drink water is from a natural source.

b) Purify it by boiling, using tablets, or filtering it

5. Natural sources of water are found in the wilderness.

a) Streams, rivers, lakes, rainwater, and certain plants

6. Knowing where to find a stream or river.

b) Listen for the sound of running water and look for green vegetation

7. Importance of purifying water before drinking it.

b) To avoid getting sick from bacteria, parasites, or other harmful germs

8. Water is still cloudy after filtering.

b) Filter it again to make it cleaner

9. Materials to use to make an emergency water filter.

a) Plastic bottle, rocks, sand, charcoal, grass or leaves

10. How charcoal helps to purify water.

b) It absorbs harmful chemicals, bacteria, and bad tastes

11. The most effective way to purify water.

b) Boil it for at least 1 minute (3 minutes at high altitudes)

12. The amount of time you should wait after adding water purification tablets before drinking.

c) 30 minutes

13. A reason for why boiling water is reliable.

b) It kills harmful bacteria, viruses, and parasites

14. What to avoid when collecting water in the wilderness.

b) Collecting from areas near dead animals or visible pollution

15. An example of why it is important to store boiled water in a clean container.

b) To prevent it from getting contaminated again

Chapter 3 Answer Key:

Multiple Choice:

1. Why fire is important in a survival situation.

b) It helps you stay warm, cook food, purify water, and signal for help

2. A material considered as tinder.

b) Dry leaves or grass

3. The shape recommended for building a fire structure.

c) Teepee

4. What to do if your fire starts to die down.

c) Add more fuel and blow gently at the base

5. Not a primitive fire-starting method.

d) Electric lighter

6. The first step in building a fire.

c) Finding a safe spot

7. How to safely extinguish a fire.

c) Pour water over it until the embers are out and the ashes are cool to the touch

8. The material used to make a fire-starter.

b) Pinecones and wax

9. What is rocket stove designed to do?

b) Burn wood very efficiently with less fuel and smoke

10. A safety tip for when using matches or lighters.

b) Strike the match away from your body

True or False:

1. Tinder is used to keep a fire burning for a long time. False

2. Blowing gently at the base of a fire helps it burn stronger by providing more oxygen. True

3. The Bow Drill method is easier to master than the Hand Drill method because it allows for greater speed and pressure. True

4. A magnifying glass can be used to start a fire using the sun's rays. True

5. What should you always do before leaving a fire site? False

Short Answer

1. Tinder - catches the initial spark or flame; Kindling - burns longer and helps ignite larger pieces of wood; Fuel - larger wood pieces that keep the fire going.

2. Pour water over the fire until all embers are out, stir the ashes to ensure there are no hot spots, and check that the ashes are cool to the touch.

3. A rocket stove uses a narrow chimney for airflow, making the fire burn hotter and using less wood. It's efficient because it produces less smoke and requires minimal fuel.

4. Example: *Bow Drill* - Uses a bow to spin a spindle in a fireboard, creating friction that produces an ember to start a fire.

5. Make sure the fire is completely out by pouring water over it and checking the ashes to ensure they are cool.

Chapter 4 Quiz Answer Key:

1. The definition of foraging.

b) Searching for wild plants that are safe to eat

2. True or False: You should only eat a plant if you are 100% sure it is safe.

True

3. What to do if you find a plant you do not recognize while foraging.

b) Ask an adult who knows about plants

4.bMatch the plant part with their description.

Leaves - c, Flowers - a, Fruits - b, Stems - d

5. True or False: Only forage near roads and industrial areas.

False

6. The use of The Universal Edibility Test.

b) To see if a plant is safe to eat

7. Name an edible plant from the list in this chapter.

(Accept any correct answer, such as Dandelion, Wild Strawberries, etc.)

8. Before eating a plant you have found, what should you do?

b) Perform the Universal Edibility Test

9. True or False: Poison Ivy, Oak, and Sumac are safe to touch and eat.

False

10. Why it is important to respect nature whilst foraging.

c) To leave enough for animals and other foragers and not harm the environment

Chapter 5 Quiz Answer Key:

1. Materials used to build a basic snare trap.

b) Sticks, vines, natural cordage, sharp stones or knife, and bait

2. When setting a snare trap, why is it important to place bait near the noose?

b) To attract the animal to the trap

3. What should you do if you catch an animal in a trap?

b) Dispatch it quickly and humanely

4. Not a sign of a rabbit's presence.

c) Small, cylindrical droppings

5. Identifying raccoon's tracks.

a) They have five toes and a somewhat hand-like appearance on the front feet

6. One way to make a simple fishing rod.

a) Use a piece of string tied to a stick

7. What to do if you feel a tug on the line.

a) Pull the rod up quickly to set the hook

8. A safe and effective way to cook fish.

b) Grill it over an open fire

9. A material not recommended for making fishing hooks.

d) Plastic straws

10. Why should you check traps regularly?

a) To avoid catching non-target animals

Chapter 6 Quiz Answer Key

Short Answer

1. A lean-to shelter is a simple structure that leans against a support like a tree or rock. It's called a "lean-to" because the structure leans on this support.

2. Three materials needed are long, sturdy branches, smaller sticks, and leaves or pine needles.

3. Checking for gaps is important to ensure the shelter stays warm and dry by preventing wind and rain from getting inside.

4. If you find cracks or weak spots in a snow shelter, reinforce them with more snow or repair the structure as needed.

5. Two types of snow shelters are igloos, which are made from snow blocks stacked in a dome shape, and quinzees, which are built by piling and hollowing out compacted snow.

Multiple Choice

1. The primary purpose of a lean-to shelter.

a) To keep you warm and dry

2. Not a material used to build a lean-to shelter.

b) Small rocks

3. The purpose of a ridgepole.

b) To act as a roof support

4. A type of snow shelter.

b) Quinzee

5. A key feature of urban shelters.

c) They need to be clean and comfortable

True or False

1. A lean-to shelter is built by leaning branches against a support like a tree or rock. True
2. For a debris hut, you should create a small entrance to keep the heat inside. True
3. Snow shelters like igloos are built using snow blocks that are stacked in a dome shape. True
4. It is not necessary to create ventilation holes in a quinzee. False
5. In an urban shelter, using bright clothing can help you be more visible to rescuers. True

Chapter 7 Quiz Answer Key

Multiple Choice

1. A first aid kit in a survival situation.

c) It helps you treat minor injuries before they become major problems

2. What makes a whistle more effective than yelling for help?

a) It uses less energy and can be heard from farther away

3. Why is a fire starter important in cold environments?

e) It can help prevent hypothermia

4. Why is it important to carry a map and compass even if you have a good sense of direction?

e) They provide more accurate information in unfamiliar areas

5. Why is it important to regularly check the expiration dates of food and water in your survival kit?

b) To ensure they are safe to eat or drink

True or False

1. First aid supplies, such as ointments and medications, can expire and should be replaced when necessary. (True/False)
2. Inspecting your survival tools, like a knife or flashlight, is unnecessary if they are stored properly. (True/False)
3. A map and compass are useful only in wilderness environments. (True/False)

4. Practicing how to pack and unpack your kit can help you become faster at finding items during an emergency. (True/False)

Chapter 8 Quiz Answer Key

Short Answer Questions:

1. Purpose of a compass.

A compass helps find your way by pointing towards magnetic north.

2. Holding a compass.

Hold the compass flat and level in your hand to allow the needle to spin freely.

3. Steps to take a bearing:

- Choose a landmark and point the compass at it.
- Rotate the bezel until the needle aligns with the north marking.
- Read the degree marking at the direction of travel arrow.
- Follow the bearing while keeping the needle aligned.

4. Interference with compass accuracy.

Metal objects and electronic devices can interfere with the compass reading.

5. Using the sun for direction:

The sun rises in the east and sets in the west. Around midday, it is generally to the south in the northern hemisphere and to the north in the southern hemisphere.

Multiple Choice Questions:

1. Part of the compass pointing north.

c) The Needle

2. Action after aligning the needle:

b) Rotate the bezel to find the bearing

3. Constellation for finding north in the northern hemisphere:

c) The Big Dipper

4. Southern hemisphere method for using an analog watch:

b) Point the 12 o'clock mark at the sun

5. Importance of combining techniques:

b) To have a backup method in case one fails

True or False Questions:

1. The needle of a compass always points to magnetic north. True

2. You should avoid using metal objects near a compass to prevent interference. True

3. In the northern hemisphere, the midpoint between the hour hand and the 12 o'clock mark on an analog watch points to true north. True

4. The sun rises in the west and sets in the east. False (The sun rises in the east and sets in the west.)

5. Using natural landmarks is an unreliable method for navigation because they can easily move. False (Natural landmarks are reliable because they don't move or change quickly.)

Chapter 9 Quiz Answer Key

Short Answer Questions

1. Type of cloud that is fluffy and whit with cotton-like appearance and usually indicates fair weather. Cumulus clouds.

2. Benefit of using a journal. By noting the types of clouds and the subsequent weather conditions, you can identify patterns and better predict future weather.

3. Behavior in birds when a storm is approaching. Birds might fly lower or seek shelter.

4. Ants building their mounds higher can indicate that rain is coming. A weather clue when ants build their mounds higher before a rainstorm.

5. What happens when a cold front is moving in. The temperature drops quickly.

Multiple Choice Questions

1. Type of cloud associated with heavy rain and storms.

c) Nimbus

2. Wind coming from the west.

c) Weather systems are moving your way

3. What should you do if you see birds flying low to the ground?

c) Prepare for a storm

4. Which type of cloud is thin and wispy, often indicating that weather might be changing?

c) Cirrus

5. If you see a sudden increase in wind speed, what might this signal?

b) Weather fronts are moving in

True or False Questions

1. Cumulus clouds are usually associated with stormy weather. False
2. An increase in cricket chirping is a sign of colder weather. False
3. The sun rising in the east and setting in the west is a good indication of where north and south are. True
4. Observing the behavior of insects can give you clues about upcoming weather changes. True
5. Rapid temperature increases generally suggest that a cold front is moving in. False

Chapter 10 Quiz Answer Key

Short Answer Questions

1. What to always be aware of in crowded areas.

Situational awareness.

2. Where should you move to avoid being trapped?

Move towards the edges.

3. Two things you should do to keep your belongings safe.

Keep bags zipped and close; avoid displaying expensive items.

4. One type of public building that can provide shelter.

Libraries, schools, community centers, police stations, fire departments, hospitals.

5. Why is it important to stick to well-lit and populated areas?

To stay safe from potential dangers and avoid isolated areas.

Multiple Choice Questions

1. A good strategy if you get separated from your group.

c) Go to a designated meeting point

2. If you see someone acting strange.

c) Trust your instincts and move away

3. A good method to attract attention.

b) Use a whistle or loud noise

4. A safe spot in urban areas that is not a public building.

a) Abandoned buildings with secure entry

True or False Questions

1. In a crowded area, you should always push through people to get out quickly. False

2. Libraries and community centers can provide shelter and assistance during emergencies. True

3. It is safer to take shortcuts through alleys when navigating the city. False

4. Keeping your bag unzipped in a crowded place is fine as long as you are alert. False

Chapter 11 Quiz Answer Key

Short Answer Questions

1. How to block an attack.

Use your forearm to block the attack.

2. Two vulnerable areas of the body that you can target in self defense.

Eyes, nose, groin.

3. One way to use keys as a defensive tool.

Hold the keys between your fingers to scratch or poke.

4. When to use self-defense techniques.

Use self-defense techniques only as a last resort.

5. A good method for de-escalating a confrontation.

Use a calm and firm voice to de-escalate the situation.

Multiple Choice Questions

1. The best way to use a book in self-defense.

b) To shield yourself from blows or push away the attacker

2. A technique involving pushing away an object or strike to redirect it safely.

b) Deflecting

3. What to do in a dangerous situation.

b) Try to avoid physical confrontation and seek help

4. Not a recommended self-defense move.

d) Shouting at the attacker

5. How staying fit can help with self-defense.

a) It improves your ability to run away quickly

True or False Questions

1. You should use self-defense techniques as a first option in any dangerous situation. False
2. Holding your keys between your fingers can be used to scratch or poke an attacker. True
3. You should always try to de-escalate a confrontation before using self-defense. True
4. Practicing self-defense with a friend or trusted adult can help build confidence and improve skills. True
5. Regular physical activity is important for staying in shape and enhancing self-defense skills. True

Chapter 12 Quiz Answer Key

Short Answer Questions

1. First step before treating any wound.

Wash your hands thoroughly with soap and water.

2. How to treat a first-degree burn.

Cool the burn with running lukewarm water for at least 10 minutes and cover it with a sterile, non-stick bandage.

3. Two signs of infection in a wound.

Redness and swelling, pus or unusual discharge.

4. When to seek adult help for a burn.

If the burn covers a large area of the body or is on sensitive areas like the face, hands, feet, or genitals.

5. What does R.I.C.E stand for?

Rest, Ice, Compression, Elevation.

Multiple Choice Questions
1. What is the proper way to clean a wound?

b) Rinse with clean water and mild soap

2. What should you use to cover a small cut or scrape?

b) Adhesive bandage

3. What is a common mistake to avoid when treating burns?

c) Applying ice or butter

4. What type of burn involves blisters and requires a non-stick bandage for protection?

b) Second-degree burn

5. When handling a blister, what should you do to protect it?

b) Apply a blister pad or clean bandage

True or False Questions

1. You should use antiseptic solution on a wound after cleaning it. True

2. It's okay to apply ice directly to a burn. False

3. When treating a sprain, you should avoid using the affected joint and follow the R.I.C.E. method. True

4. Blisters should be popped to relieve pain and prevent infection. False

5. You should seek adult help if a burn covers a large area or is on sensitive parts of the body. True

Chapter 13 Quiz Answer Key

Short Answer Questions

1. Two benefits of having a family survival weekend.

Building teamwork and communication skills and strengthening family bonds.

2. Name a place where you can have a family survival weekend if you're looking for a bit more of a challenge than your backyard.

Local park or camping site.

3. Name at least two essential items to pack.

Examples include tent, tarp, ropes, matches, or a first aid kit.

4. The purpose of debriefing after a family survival weekend.

To review what you did, what you learned, and how to improve for future practice.

5. Two specific survival challenges you could include in your family survival weekend.

Examples include building a shelter using natural materials, starting a campfire, or navigating with a compass.

Multiple Choice Questions

1. A suitable location for a beginner family survival weekend.

b) Your backyard

2. The first step in safely starting a fire in your backyard.

c) Use a fire pit or fire-safe container

3. What to do if you are practicing fire-starting and the kindling catches fire.

b) Make sure an adult is supervising

4. What should you use to cover the frame of a lean-to shelter.

b) Leaves, grass, or other natural materials

5. What should you discuss during a debrief.

b) What went well and what could be improved

True or False Questions

1. A family survival weekend can help build teamwork and communication skills. True

2. It's okay to use ice or butter on a burn during a survival practice. False

3. You should always have an adult present when starting or tending a fire. True

4. Creating a scavenger hunt for edible plants can be a fun and educational activity. True

5. During the debriefing, you should only talk about the things that went well and not discuss any challenges faced. False

www.ingramcontent.com/pod-product-compliance
Lightning Source LLC
Chambersburg PA
CBHW051351070526
44584CB00025B/3723